Hydroponics
Questions & Answers
~for Successful Growing

Dr. Resh is an international consultant on
hydroponics and author of the landmark work,
Hydroponic Food Production,
as well as
Hydroponic Home Food Gardens
and
Hydroponic Tomatoes for the Home Gardener.

Hydroponics
Questions & Answers
~ for Successful Growing

Problem-Solving Conversations with

Howard M. Resh

Woodbridge Press ❖ *Santa Barbara*

Published and Distributed by

Woodbridge Press Publishing Company
Post Office Box 209
Santa Barbara, California 93102

Copyright © 1998 by Howard M. Resh

Printed in the United States of America.
Distributed simultaneously in Canada.

Library of Congress Cataloging-in-Publication Data:

Resh, Howard M.
Hydroponics, Questions and Answers :   problem-solving
   conversations with Howard M. Resh.
        p.   cm.
Includes Index.
ISBN 0-88007-220-2   (alk. paper)
1. Hydroponics—Miscellanea.   I. Title
SB126.5.R486   1998   98-6582
631.5'85—dc21   CIP

Disclaimer:

While I have attempted to present the most up-to-date information available in answering these questions, techniques change with new solutions to problems. New products are introduced and uses of existing products may be modified in the light of new procedures. *In addition, government regulations change in the* **approval and application recommendations** *of existing and new pesticides and biological agents.* Please check your local regulations.

   Neither the author nor the publisher can be held responsible for exact pesticide and biological agent application rates, as these come from third parties. The grower must always check the label of the product he is using in determining the correct application rates and safe procedures. Rates and methods for similar products from different manufacturers may vary.

   The information given herein is to be used as a general guideline. The reader is expected to obtain specific information from the sources of products being used, and to determine specific cultural practices, through growing experience, under his or her particular conditions, as well as to be familiar with legal requirements of his particular state, province, or other regulatory jurisdiction.   —*The Author*

Table of Contents

Skillful hydroponic growing brings many rewards, aesthetic and material. The prize example above is pak choi (baby bok choy), grown in the greenhouses of the F. W. Armstrong Ranch, Oakview, California.

Introduction

In the sciences there are always more questions than answers. Hydroponics is no exception. However, as hydroponics is an applied science, experience is gained each time it is used as a growing technique. New problems and questions arise with each type of soilless culture and with each crop grown. In fact, hydroponic growing of similar crops under different environmental conditions creates new problems. There are many variables in the growing of crops which producers encounter from one day to the next. Some cause problems, while others have little effect. The grower's challenge is to closely observe these variabilities and identify their effects on plant growth. If the effect is injurious to plant health the grower must take steps to correct it immediately to prevent stress and additional harm to the plants.

Hydroponic culture minimizes some of the problems of plant culture, but there are still problems and many answers to be discovered.

The purpose of this book is to review many questions associated with hydroponic culture and to offer useful suggestions. The questions relate to hydroponic systems, plant varieties, plant nutrition, plant culture, plant disease and pest management, environmental factors, optimum ranges, production and marketing. Recommendations come from experiences of others and myself over the past twenty years of hydroponic growing. I will approach these questions under various topics for quick reference within a subject.

Hydroponics *vs.* Other Cultures

1. Many people tell me that hydroponics is any culture using an artificial medium. Is that correct?

Hydroponics is defined by word meanings as "water working," a definition derived from the Greek words hydro=water and ponos=labor. So defined, hydroponic culture is the culture of plants, using only water as a substrate, or base, with the addition of plant essential nutrients. No substrate other than the water is used. This definition restricts true hydroponics to water culture—in systems such as nutrient film technique (NFT), the deep flow or raft culture system, aeroponic systems and possibly ebb-and-flow culture of seedlings in growing cubes.

2. If "true hydroponics" is water culture, what are the other cultures using artificial media?

Other cultures using artificial media, as well as true hydroponics, are usually included in the term "soilless culture," The growing of plants using substrates, or media, other than soil. Such substrates include, but are not restricted to: water (hydroponics), sand, gravel, haydite (fired clay), pumice, perlite, vermiculite, charcoal, peat, moss, bark, sawdust, wood chips, rice hulls, peanut hulls, plastic foams, styrofoam, petroleum based rigid foam-like cubes, rockwool and any mixtures containing a number of these products. Any medium that provides adequate oxygenation, water retention, good drainage, and is relatively sterile and inert is suitable for soilless culture. Note that while soilless culture includes hydroponics, hydroponic culture, by strict definition, consists of water culture without any other substrate. Both cultures use a nutrient solution to provide the plant essential elements. The choice of medium depends upon availability, cost and the plants to be grown.

Thus, in general, when we speak about hydroponics we include all forms of soilless culture. I feel that this is fine, as the cultural techniques are basically the same for all soilless cultures in that the management of the nutrient solution is key to its success.

3. Many people argue with me that hydroponics is not organic. Do you consider hydroponics as organic or inorganic?

This is a real "red herring" question. I like to argue that greenhouse hydroponic culture is almost organic. The biggest argument between organic and non-organic centers around the use of synthetic pesticides. Pest control in greenhouse hydroponics is over 90 percent by biological agents. Pest control through integrated pest management (IPM) is the widely accepted method. This includes the use of predatory agents, which kill the pests. Some soft pesticides such as soaps (M-Pede), extracts from plants (Azatin, Neemix), bacteria (Dipel, Vectobac), fungi (Mycoprop, BotaniGard) and others are safe to use with biological agents in controlling outbreaks of infestations without damaging the predatory-prey balances. This places the hydroponic produce in "pesticide-free" status, but organic growers argue that it is still not organic due to the use of chemical fertilizers.

To be truly organic hydroponic culture should use organic sources of nutrients such as fish fertilizers, sea plant extracts, and other "natural" fertilizers, not refined ones. Many of these organic fertilizers are suitable for field crops as the soil always provides a certain level of nutrition for the plants. Hydroponic culture, on the other hand, begins without any nutrients in the substrate and generally inadequate amounts in the raw water. However, raw water often has calcium and magnesium carbonates, iron, boron, zinc and other microelements. Their levels are generally non-optimum and therefore the water requires additional nutrients. Sometimes levels of micronutrients can be too high and will have to be removed from the water by reverse osmosis. Organic nutrient formulations are available for hydroponics, but often they are lacking in several elements, which will have to be added from other fertilizers, and they may be too costly for larger, commercial greenhouses. I am presently working on the development of an organic complete nutrient source from prehistoric composts that have not formed into coal. The material is steeped with water for a 24-hour period to remove the nutrients in a concentrated form. It then is prepared as a concentrated two-part liquid.

However, I suggest that inorganic fertilizers act in the same manner as organic ones in terms of plant uptake. All have to break down into ionic forms and attach to soil colloids (in the case of soil culture) and then are released into the water surrounding the plant roots (which is the same as the nutrient solution of hydroponics). Ionic exchange then takes place between the plant roots and the nutrient solution (or soil solution in soil culture). Physiologically the plant experiences no difference between the soil solution or nutrient solution ionic exchange. Therefore, I suggest that if the plants are grown pesticide free, hydroponically, it can be argued that they are really organically grown.

4. People tell me that hydroponics is the answer to the food problems of the world. What do you think is the future of hydroponics?

Hydroponics has its niche, but I would not say it is the answer to the food problems of the world. Its primary function is in the growing of fresh, perishable crops under intensive culture. Hydroponics has become a key factor in "controlled environment agriculture" (CEA). CEA is the growing of plants for agriculture in structures—generally greenhouses—which enable us to control the environment of the enclosed crop. In addition to greenhouses, other structures such as large warehouses having artificial lighting may be used. This may be extended to highly sophisticated systems like "Controlled Ecological Life Support Systems" designed for the growing of plants in zero gravity, in NASA's space station program. Hydroponic culture is the component of these systems providing plants with water and essential elements.

Hydroponically grown products are recognized as having superior flavor and high quality, free of pesticides and disease-causing organisms. In many areas of the world such as Mexico, Central and South America, where human diseases like dysentery and cholera spread by contaminated water used in irrigating crops, hydroponic culture is becoming the method of choice for providing safe, clean vegetables. This is particularly true for fresh salad crops, including tomatoes, cucumbers, peppers, lettuce, radish, watercress, herbs and sprouts, all eaten without cooking. With consumer confidence in hydroponic products, the market for hydroponic vegetables is expanding rapidly. We will find in the near future many more commercial hydroponic greenhouse and cold frames established in developing countries as the politics and economies stabilize, creating an established middle class of people who will be looking for high-quality fresh vegetables. They will be willing and able to pay a premium price for the superior quality of hydroponic vegetables, as is the case in Venezuela.

In areas like North America and Europe, where a large middle class of people demand high quality vegetables, very large greenhouse hydroponic operations are developing, especially in areas with high solar radiation and adequate water. I see a prosperous future in commercial greenhouses, concentrating on a large scale in the sunbelt areas of the southwestern United States and in Mexico to supply the North American demand for fresh salad crops. In Europe, such concentrations of large greenhouse operations have developed in Spain (and also in Morocco) to supply the European markets.

As efficient, low-cost, artificial lighting is developed, emphasis may shift to the use of large warehouses in or near the central core of cities, to grow low-profile crops such as strawberries, spinach, lettuce, herbs, etc. These may be tiered on shelves. Such growing of very high-density crops, efficiently utilizing the vertical space, can be automated for planting and harvesting, thus reducing production costs. Crops such as tomatoes, peppers, cucumbers, etc., which themselves grow vertically and require much higher light intensity than the leafy crops will be more difficult and costly to grow outside the areas of naturally high solar radiation.

Of course, in space, growing crops hydroponically is the only practical method. This production, however, will serve to provide fresh vegetables to the workers of the space station itself and not be of any significance in relation to "the world food problem." However, technology developed for the space program may have application to hydroponic growing on earth. For example, new technology in artificial lighting, water purification, disease and pest control, recirculation of nutrients and the management of long-term use of the nutrient solution will all benefit commercial hydroponics here on earth.

Site Selection

5. People tell me that it is important to orient my greenhouse so that the crop rows will run north-south. How important is this orientation and for what crops?

Whether or not the orientation of a greenhouse is important for crop growth depends upon the crop. Low profile crops do not cast significant mutual shading among the plants. Vine crops growing vertically in the greenhouse, such as tomatoes, peppers and cucumbers, shade adjacent rows. To balance the amount of shading from one row to another the rows need to be oriented from north to south. In large operations, rows of greenhouses should be oriented in the same direction, as crop rows are normally parallel to the gutters. Of course, as you approach the equator this effect becomes less significant, as the sun is located more or less overhead. The shading effect is most pronounced during winter months in northern latitudes when the angle of incidence of the sun is very low. If rows are oriented from east to west, the most southern row of plants will receive most sunlight, with adjacent rows on the northern side receiving substantially less sunlight. This effect will be at a maximum from 10:00 AM to 3:00 PM, the period when the sunlight is of sufficient intensity to be of photosynthetic value.

6. I have been told by other growers that greenhouses use a lot of electricity and that it is a significant cost of production. Do you have some pointers on electrical service?

The amount of amperage of electricity is a function of the size of the greenhouse operation and the number of electrical components. The more fans, pumps, lights, etc. installed the more amperage will be needed. One general rule, however, is to have three-phase power, especially for a large operation. This enables the motors of pumps, fans, etc. to be operated on 220 volts or higher, which is more efficient and less expensive.

7. I have heard people say that if you are growing hydroponically you do not need much water. How much water do the plants use?

Availability of water is critical in greenhouse location. Even if you plan on growing low profile crops, I would suggest that you base your planning for a water supply upon the water needs of vine crops, even if you aren't, at first, going to grow vine crops. Then you will not be short in the future should you find it necessary to change your crop according to market demand and prices, or personal interest.

A general rule for water consumption by vine crops is 1 liter (1 quart)/square foot of greenhouse area/day, during maximum usage of summer months with mature plants. Add to this volume the need for water in cooling pads, sprinklers, and water usage in the greenhouse operation itself, or packing and office facilities if those are involved.

Thinking of commercial operations, one acre of greenhouses would need at least 50,000 to 60,000 liters (about 15,000 gallons) per day. This is equivalent to a well capacity of 21 gpm (gallons per minute) over a 12-hour period. Most wells of an 8-inch casing should be able to pump 300 gpm or more as long as the drawdown on the water is met by the underlying water table. The capacity of available water can be increased by use of large storage tanks, filled from the well pump 24-hours per day. The greenhouses are then supplied with water from the storage tank by a booster pump.

8. I have heard people say that if water can be used for drinking it can easily be used to grow plants. How important is water quality?

It is not necessarily true that drinking water can be used by plants; some drinking water may have higher than acceptable levels of micronutrients. Before formulating your nutrient solution you have to know what is in the raw water. A reputable laboratory must be called upon to test the raw water for all macro- and microelements. The elements include nitrate-nitrogen, ammonium-nitrogen, phosphorous, potassium, calcium, magnesium, sulfate-sulfur, iron, chloride, manganese, copper, boron, zinc, molybdenum, fluoride, and sodium. In addition, test for the following elements which could be toxic, or accumulate in your crop, if present in relatively high levels: chromium, lead, aluminum, cadmium, nickel, strontium, barium, vanadium, cobalt and tin. It would also be prudent to test for biological contaminants such as *E. coli.* If any of the microelements are in excess, it will be necessary to remove them by water treatment, such as reverse osmosis. If biological contaminant counts exceed acceptable levels, they will have to be reduced through chlorination and filtration processes.

High levels of microelements can be phytotoxic, while the presence of biological contaminants is not acceptable. Remember that hydroponically grown vegetables must be free of any disease-causing organisms. They are marketed as being high quality and clean, and therefore command a premium price.

Plant Nutrition

9. If my nutrient solution is missing an essential element can this harm the plant? What is an essential element?

An essential element is one that the plant cannot do without (it cannot complete its life cycle), no other element can substitute for it and it is an essential constituent for a plant process (metabolite). There are 16 essential elements. According to the relative quantities required they are classified as macroelements and microelements (trace or minor elements). If the plants do not have all 16 of these elements, they will not develop properly.

10. The terms major and macroelements confuse me. What are the macroelements and their sources?

There are nine macroelements: hydrogen (H), carbon (C), oxygen (O), nitrogen (N), phosphorus (P), potassium (K), calcium (Ca), magnesium (Mg) and sulfur (S). Carbon comes from the atmosphere in the form of carbon dioxide. Hydrogen comes from the water, as does oxygen. The remaining six must be added to the water as fertilizers as part of the nutrient solution.

11. What are the microelements?

The microelements include iron (Fe), manganese (Mn), boron (B), copper (Cu), zinc (Zn), molybdenum (Mo), and chlorine (Cl). Nickel (Ni) is thought to be an essential element, but as yet not proven to be one.

12. There are many scientific documents showing that other elements exist in plants. What other elements accumulate in plants and what are their functions?

A number of microelements serve a function in plants or accumulate in plant tissues, but have not met the criteria of being essential. Silicone (Si), aluminum (Al), cobalt (Co), vanadium (V), selenium (Se), platinum (Pt), lead (Pb) and others accumulate in plants. Silicone adds strength to plant cells, giving resistance to fungal infection, and is added to the nutrient solution as potassium silicate for the growing of cucumbers. Lead can be taken up, reaching levels toxic to animals or people eating the plants. Such has been the case with grasses grown in high traffic areas when cars used leaded gasoline. This was one of the reasons for eliminating lead from gasoline, to reduce its presence in the environment.

Many of these additional elements are found in raw water. They are also present as impurities at very low levels in most fertilizers, and you add them to the nutrient solution when you use these fertilizers. If your raw water contains more than the acceptable levels of these trace elements it will be necessary to treat the water to reduce or remove them.

13. What is the source of oxygen for the plants?

Often growers overlook some of the basic functions of the nutrient solution. The nutrient solution is the principal source of oxygen to plant roots. This is termed dissolved oxygen. Oxygen is needed in metabolism, the chemical reactions of photosynthesis and respiration of plant growth and development. One of the by-products of root respiration is carbon dioxide. This may be carried in the nutrient solution in addition to other waste metabolites.

14. I understand that plants need oxygen, but what are the effects of low dissolved oxygen levels in the nutrient solution?

If the dissolved oxygen level in the nutrient solution is low, the uptake of essential elements by roots will be reduced. Once the uptake falls below optimum levels stress will occur and result eventually in mineral deficiencies, which will reduce productivity. One of the most common deficiencies encountered is blossom-end-rot (BER), a calcium deficiency brought on by the inability of the plant to take up calcium, even if the calcium level in the nutrient solution is normally adequate. At the same time, root die back may occur, causing wilting of the plants and increased disease infection.

15. I use an air pump in my tank to add oxygen to the nutrient solution. What other methods will add oxygen to the nutrient solution?

The addition of oxygen to the nutrient solution is particularly important in recirculating systems, as the oxygen level will be reduced as the solution passes by the roots of the plants. Add oxygen to the nutrient solution 24 hours per day by use of an air pump connected to large air stones (normally used in fish culture) set at the bottom of the tank. Also, as the water returns to the tank it should fall free. This will oxygenate the solution. A bypass located next to the pump at the tank can constantly circulate solution, adding oxygen as it falls back to the tank. In NFT systems the solution flow rate within the channels should be a minimum of one to 2 liters (¼ - ½ gallon) per minute.

16. My tomatoes are now mature, producing fruit. Does the age of the plant and other factors affect the nutrient uptake?

As plants mature they require more water and nutrients. It is important to understand that water uptake is closely tied to mineral uptake. As plants mature under optimal light and temperature conditions they will consume a lot of water through evapotranspiration. The higher the water loss rate, the greater the pull on water through the plant and increased root absorption. This is favorable to mineral absorption. With a high metabolic rate, the demand for water and minerals will be high, adding photosynthates, resulting in rapid growth and development. Under low light levels, mature plants may grow faster than is optimum for fruit production, forming thin, leggy and excessively leafy plants. Such vegetative plants produce low fruit yields. In this case, the nutrient solution formulation needs to be adjusted in order to slow vegetative growth.

17. My nutrient formulation was unbalanced, producing symptoms on the plants. Would you comment on nutritional disorders?

A nutritional disorder in a plant is a response of the plant to a deficiency or excess of a mineral element. This plant response is due to an upset in at least one physiological process as a result of stress. If the stress continues, the abnormal growth will produce symptoms. Initially, these symptoms are specific to the mineral disorder and can be used to identify the element causing the problem. If the level of essential element or other factor preventing its uptake is not corrected quickly, uptake of other elements may be interfered with, causing compounded effects in the plant, resulting in complex symptoms not specific to any one nutrient disorder. Eventual death of the plant can occur if corrective steps are not taken.

18. I have had some problems with my nutrient formulation and now symptoms appear on the plants that do not fit those of any one element. What has happened here?

As mentioned above, a deficiency of one element will often lead to a deficiency of another. That is, a deficiency in an element may be antagonistic to the uptake of another. For this reason, it is very important to correct nutrient imbalances immediately. For instance, a boron deficiency can lead to a deficiency in calcium. Calcium deficiency may cause a potassium disorder and vice versa.

19. Initially, symptoms on my tomatoes were similar in color, but as days passed, many other problems of yellowing and browning occurred. How can I keep track of what is happening?

Nutritional disorders produce symptoms on specific areas of plants, according to the mobility of the elements. Most essential elements are classified as mobile or immobile. That is, if a deficiency occurs within the plant, can the plant retranslocate (move) the element from where it was originally deposited (older lower leaves) to the actively growing area of the plant, the younger leaves? If so, the element is mobile. Symptoms will first appear on older (lower) leaves, as the plant shifts the element to the younger (upper) part of the growing tip. Immobile elements are those that are not retranslocated. As a result, first symptoms will appear on the upper part of the plant. The mobile elements are nitrogen, phosphorus, potassium, magnesium and zinc. The immobile elements include calcium, sulfur, iron, boron, copper and manganese.

20. I understand that the acidic or basic nature of the nutrient solution must meet certain levels. What is pH and its effect on plants?

The pH value is a measure of acidity or alkalinity of the nutrient solution. It measures the ratio of H^+ to OH^- ions in solution. One unit change in pH is a 10-fold change in H^+ ion concentration, as pH is a logarithmic function. The pH scale ranges from 1 to 10, with 7.0 as neutral. Most plants need a pH level between 6.0 and 7.0 for optimum nutrient uptake. The grower must determine what is the optimum pH for a specific crop and then keep the pH of the nutrient solution at that level. The pH of the nutrient solution must be checked at least several times a day—or continuously if the greenhouse is equipped with computerized equipment.

21. I am using a small hand-held meter to test pH. What other methods of testing pH are available?

The pH may be tested with simple indicator papers or solutions, or, with various degrees of sophistication, pH meters. For small greenhouse operations not having a computer system it is adequate to test with indicator paper or a relatively simple portable tester. Indicator papers of various pH ranges are available. Use those having a range of 4.0 to 7.0 in increments of 0.2 to 0.3 units. A package of 100 with a color chart costs about $15. A pH indicator solution kit such as the Fisher Universal pH Indicator Kit, covering a pH range from 4.0 to 10.0, costs about $40. Simple hand-held meters start at about $50. A problem with the inexpensive models is that they lose accuracy and must be calibrated often, with several pH buffer solutions. Other, more accurate, meters (which can be transported to the greenhouse, but with care), cost from $250 to $400. They also must be calibrated with buffer solutions. Other units, which are monitors, should be attached to the downstream main line from the nutrient tank or injector system. These give a continuous readout and can operate an alarm and/or other device for feedback to a computer should the pH exceed or fall below a preset range. These pH monitors cost $900 and up, depending upon their precision and functions.

22. If my pH is too low or too high what are the safe ways of adjusting it?

There are two situations with the pH level: the solution will be too acidic or too basic. For example, with tomatoes, if the pH is below the optimum range from 6.3 to 6.5, you must raise it with a base. You may use either potassium hydroxide (KOH) or sodium hydroxide (NaOH). I prefer to use potassium hydroxide as it contains potassium, a useful plant nutrient, rather than sodium hydroxide containing sodium, a nonessential element. Also, raw water may have high levels of sodium not favorable to plant growth, so we do not want to add to it. Dissolve KOH in water before adding it to the nutrient solution, as it is very concentrated and can precipitate if not added slowly while mixing the solution.

If the pH is high, you must lower it with an acid. Some acids commonly used to lower pH are: nitric acid, sulfuric acid and phosphoric acid. These acids are purchased in concentrated form of 42 percent, 66 percent and 75 percent, respectively. Muriatic (hydrochloric) acid (HCl) can also be used but it adds chlorine that may already be present at non-optimal levels in the water, so it is preferable to use one of the others. Always add acid to water while stirring; that is, add it directly to the nutrient solution or to your acid stock solution tank after filling the tank three-quarters full with water. *These acids and potassium hydroxide produce toxic vapors and burn the skin, so you must wear an approved respirator, plastic/rubber gloves,*

*apron and eye goggles, and certainly follow the directions
on the label of the product you are using.*

23. I am measuring the conductivity of my nutrient solution. What do these reading represent?

The measurement of electrical conductivity of your
solution indicates the total dissolved solutes (TDS) in the
solution. The total dissolved solutes include all the elements that are present in the raw water and those you
added in the form of fertilizers. Electrical conductivity (EC)
is a quantitative value indicating the amount of ions (free
radicals such as H^+, K^+, Mg^{++}, Ca^{++}, Cl^-, $PO_4^{\equiv}$, $SO_4^=$, OH^-,
etc.) that are present in solution and are capable of con-
ducting an electrical charge. The negative ions are called
anions, as they are attracted to the positive pole of a mag-
netic charge, and the positive ions are termed cations,
attracted to the negative pole.

Electrical conductivity instruments detect the conductivity in millimhos (mMho) across a solution distance of
one centimeter. The desired range of EC is usually from
2.00 to 4.00 mMho/cm. Electrical conductivity (EC) varies with the concentration of elements present and the
chemical composition of the nutrient solution. For example, ammonium sulfate conducts twice as much electricity as calcium nitrate and three times that of magnesium sulfate. While this relationship exists between TDS
and EC, it is important to realize that it does not indicate
the concentration of individual elements. Therefore, while
the EC of a solution may be optimum the solution ionic
ratios may not be and a nutritional disorder could occur.
Other testing is needed to determine the exact concentration of individual elements.

24. The term parts per million (ppm) is used with nutrient formulations. Could you explain this to me in simple terms?

This is the common unit for measuring the concentration of elements in nutrient solutions. It is imperative to understand the use of parts per million in order to make up any nutrient formulation. One ppm is one part of an entity in one million parts of another. For example, one milligram (mg) of elemental iron in one million mg of water. It is equivalent to one mg per liter of water (mg/l). Nutrient formulations are expressed in ppm or mg/l of each of the element constituents. This concept is basic to calculating your fertilizer weights required in a given volume of water to arrive at the desired nutrient solution formulation.

25. The term milliequivalents per liter (me/l) is often used with solution analysis. What is its relation to parts per million?

Milliequivalents is another unit used to measure the concentration of ions in a solution. However, unlike ppm, takes into consideration the valency (number of charges) on the ions. There is a relationship between ppm and me/l: me/l = ppm /equivalent wt (eq) or ppm = me/l × eq. Equivalent weight of a compound is the molecular or atomic weight divided by its valency. It is important to be able to make this conversion, as some laboratories will provide test results in me/l and you need to convert this unit to ppm if you normally use parts per million in your nutrient formulations.

26. People often use the term "kilopascals" when referring to pressure, such as vapor pressure deficit when speaking of humidity. What is the relationship to pounds per square inch?

Here are the conversion factors: one kPa = 0.145 lb./ sq. in.; or conversely: one lb./sq. in. = 6.9 kPa.

27. I realize that laboratory analyses are important. What kind of laboratory testing should the grower do?

In addition to the daily monitoring of pH and EC, the grower must periodically send nutrient solution and plant tissue samples to a reputable laboratory for analysis. When initially making up a nutrient solution according to theoretical calculations of a given nutrient formulation, some adjustments will be required to make up the differences between the levels of elements actually in the solution and those calculated to be there. Take samples weekly, adjusting the formulation based upon laboratory results, until the theoretical and actual formulations differ by no more than 5 percent. You must have all the macro- and microelements tested. Differences between the theoretical and actual formulations exist due to varying fertilizer purities and solubilities.

Plant tissue analysis will indicate the levels of nutrients within the plant. It indicates the elements and their concentrations being actually taken up from the nutrient solution. These levels can be compared with tables of optimum levels for a given plant to determine if some problem exists. If imbalances are present, they could be a result of reactions occurring in the nutrient solution (nonoptimum pH), lack of inert substrate, or environmental factors unfavorable to plant health (poor light, low carbon dioxide, etc.).

28. When having a nutrient solution analysis done, what should I have tested?

When submitting your sample for testing ask for the following: pH, total dissolved solutes, EC, nitrate-nitrogen, ammonium-nitrogen, sulfate-sulfur, phosphorus, potassium, calcium as calcium carbonate, magnesium as magnesium carbonate, iron, copper, manganese, zinc, boron, molybdenum, sodium and chloride. Often laboratories will offer complete package elements including the above as well as nickel, lead, chromium, cadmium, aluminum, strontium, barium, vanadium, beryllium, tin, and cobalt. It is good to know these also on a raw water test to determine if there may be any possible toxicity of your water.

29. There are many fertilizers on the market. Choosing the correct ones is a mystery to me. Are there special fertilizers to use with hydroponics?

Fertilizers of highest purity and solubility must be used to readily dissolve into water. Many of the fertilizers used in soil culture are of low purity and solubility. In fact, with soils it is generally better to use a fertilizer that is lower in solubility so that it will be leached more slowly, not moving so rapidly through the soil and thus being lost to the plants. In hydroponics the contrary is true; we want fertilizers that will dissolve quickly in water to form the nutrient solution. The more soluble fertilizers of higher quality are also more expensive. For the macronutrients we cannot use laboratory grade chemicals, as they are very costly. However, that is possible for some micronutrients, as we require very small amounts. The fertilizer and its source are important in your choice.

For macronutrients use the following:

Potassium nitrate ("K-Power" brand from Israel)
-Supplies potassium, nitrate-nitrogen
Calcium nitrate ("Viking Ship" brand, "Solution Grade")
-Supplies calcium, nitrate-nitrogen
Monopotassium phosphate
-Supplies potassium, phosphorus
Potassium sulfate ("GSL" brand-soluble fines)
-Supplies potassium, sulfate
Magnesium sulfate
-Supplies magnesium, sulfate
Ammonium nitrate ("ICI"- has no plasticizer)
-Supplies ammonium- & nitrate-nitrogen

For micronutrients use:

Iron chelate (FeEDTA or FeEDDHA) (10-13% Fe)
-Supplies iron
Manganese chelate (MnEDTA) (5% liquid)
-Supplies manganese
Manganese sulfate -Supplies manganese
Manganese chloride -Supplies manganese
Zinc chelate (ZnEDTA) (14% powder)
-Supplies zinc
Zinc sulfate -Supplies zinc
Zinc chloride -Supplies zinc
Boric acid -Supplies boron
Copper sulfate -Supplies copper
Ammonium molybdate -Supplies molybdenum
Sodium molybdate -Supplies molybdenum

A more in-depth presentation of nutrient formulations and calculations may be found in the book *Hydroponic Food Production* (Howard M. Resh, Woodbridge Press, Santa Barbara, CA 93102).

30. I have difficulty dissolving potassium sulfate. What can I do to get it to dissolve better?

First, use hot water. Dissolve it, separately from other elements, in 5-gallon (20-liter) buckets. Cant off the top solution and repeat the process numerous times until it dissolves. Also, use the fine white powder (like sugar) form. I have found that GSL brand's "soluble fines" is the best for me.

31. I find it very difficult to convert ppm of an element into pounds per gallon of nutrient solution. Is there a simple method that a layman could understand?

Most people have a difficult time converting their nutrient formulation into actual weight in a given tank volume. The calculations are best explained by using an example. To avoid confusion it is best to make your calculations in metric units and later convert to the foot-pound-second (fps) system. To deal with these conversions it is a good idea to purchase and use a small booklet of tables of conversion factors, weights and measures. Here are a few factors that you need to use:

> 1 ppm = 1 milligram/liter (mg/l) (weight/volume)
> 1 U.S. gallon (gal) = 3.785 liters (l)
> 1000 grams (gm) = 1 kilogram (kg)
> 1 kg = 2.2 pound (lb)
> 1 lb = 16 ounces (oz)
> 1 oz = 28.35 gm
> 1000 mg = gm

It is important to understand the principle of atomic and molecular weights in calculating the amount of an element present in the fertilizer you wish to use. The fraction of an element in the fertilizer is needed to calculate the amount of the fertilizer required. Here are some atomic weights of some elements:

Boron (B) 10.81
Calcium (Ca) 40.08
Copper (Cu) 63.54
Hydrogen (H) 1.01
Iron (Fe) 55.85
Magnesium (Mg) 24.31
Manganese (Mn) 54.94
Molybdenum (Mo) 95.94
Nitrogen (N) 14.01
Oxygen (O) 16.00
Phosphorus (P) 30.97
Potassium (K) 39.10
Sulfur (S) 32.06
Zinc (Zn) 65.37

Now, for an example. If we require 200 ppm of Ca in our nutrient formulation, using calcium nitrate:

$Ca(NO_3)_2$
Atomic weights:　　$Ca = 40.08$
　　　　　　　　　$N = 14.01$
　　　　　　　　　$O = 16.00$

Molecular weight of calcium nitrate:
$40.08 + 2 \times 14.01 + 6 \times 16.00 = 164.1$

(1 atom of Ca + 2 atoms of N + 6 atoms of O)

Fraction of Ca in calcium nitrate: $40.08/164.1 = 0.244$ That is, 164 mg of calcium nitrate contains 40 mg of calcium, or there is 0.244 mg of Ca in 1 mg of calcium nitrate. We need 200 ppm or 200 mg of Ca in 1 liter of water. *How much calcium nitrate do we require?*

$200 \times 1/0.244 = 820$ mg of calcium nitrate (each 1 mg of calcium nitrate contains 0.244 mg of Ca).

Therefore, 820 mg of calcium nitrate dissolved in 1 liter of water gives us 200 ppm of Ca. This assumes the calcium nitrate is 100 percent pure. If not, it must be adjusted. Normally, calcium nitrate is only 90 percent pure; therefore, we must adjust as follows:

$$820 \times 100\% / 90\% = 911 \text{ mg of calcium nitrate}$$

Calcium nitrate also contains nitrogen (N). Calculate the amount of nitrogen in the fertilizer, using the unadjusted amount of 820 mg/l:

$$820 \times 2 \times 14.01 \text{ (2 atoms of N)} / 164.1 = 140 \text{ mg}$$

That is, 911 mg (adjusted) of calcium nitrate provides 200 mg of Ca and 140 mg of N.

Now calculate the amount needed for the tank volume. For example, if our tank is 1000 US gallons:

Number of liters in tank: $1000 \times 3.785 = 3785$ liters.

For every liter we need 911 mg of calcium nitrate; therefore, in 3785 liters we need:

$911 \times 3785 = 3{,}448{,}135$ mg or 3448 gm (1000 mg = 1 gm) = 3.448 kg (1000 gm = 1 kg)

Now convert to the fps system:

Convert kilograms to pounds using 1 kg = 2.2 lb: $3.448 \times 2.2 = 7.59$ lb.

Convert the fraction of pounds to ounces: $0.59 \times 16 = 9.4$ oz.

Finally, 7 lb, 9.4 oz of calcium nitrate in 1000 gallons of water will give us 200 ppm of Ca and 140 ppm of N.

Proceed with all the other elements in the formulation and their appropriate fertilizers in the same manner.

32. The bag of iron chelate that I purchased indicates 13 percent iron. How much will be required to give 5 ppm of iron in a 1000-gallon tank?

If your fertilizer container indicates a percentage of an element, it is easier to calculate from that than from basic principles. *Here's how you do it:*

You need 5 mg/l (5 mg in every liter of water) of elemental iron. Each mg of iron chelate gives:

1mg × 13% = 0.13 mg of iron or: 100 mg of iron chelate gives 13 mg of iron

For 5 mg of iron you need: 5 × 100/13 = 38.5 mg of iron chelate.

That is, 38.5 mg of iron chelate in 1 liter of water gives 5 ppm of iron. For 1000 gallons the amount of iron chelate required is:

1000 × 3.785 = 3785 liters

Thus, 3785 × 38.5 = 145,722 mg or 146 gm.

33. After making up my nutrient solution I found a white powder settled to the bottom of the tank. What is this and how could it be prevented?

This is precipitation, which occurs when several compounds react and form an insoluble salt that settles to the bottom. This may be prevented using the following procedures: (1) Fill the nutrient tank to one-quarter full with water before adding dissolved fertilizers. (2) Dissolve each fertilizer separately in 5-gallon buckets (hot water works better than cold) or a mixing tank before adding it to the tank. If you use buckets, use a number of them, adding about ¼ full of fertilizers in each, then add water stirring at the same time. Let the fertilizer that does not dissolve settle to the bottom of the buckets before pouring the liquid off the top into the tank. Repeat a number of times until no solid fertilizer is left in the buckets. Add more water to the tank at the same time that you pour in the dissolved fertilizer. (3) Agitation of the tank solution while making it up will help also.

The following sequence in adding fertilizers to the tank is important to prevent precipitation—add them in the following order: potassium nitrate, calcium nitrate, ammonium nitrate, monopotassium phosphate, potassium sulfate, magnesium sulfate, iron chelate and the micronutrients. Fill the tank to at least half before adding the sulfates; not too much as you will need to add a lot more when adding the dissolved potassium sulfate. After adding the sulfates, fill the tank to within 50 gallons of final volume. Then adjust the pH to 6.5, using nitric acid before adding iron chelate and the micronutrients. Fill the tank to the final volume and adjust the pH.

It is also helpful to agitate the solution in the tank constantly, using a circulation pump and an aeration pump.

34. I understand that different crops require different nutrient formulations and that you must use an optimum formula for your plants. How important is this?

Individual crops do require specific formulations. It is important to understand which formulae are suitable for your crop and at the same time be aware that the formula for a specific crop needs to be changed with the plant's growth cycle. The changes of your formulation will assist in the control of vegetative growth of the plants in order to keep them productive. An optimum formulation is the one you must develop for your plants under your specific conditions. That requires constant adjustment, with changes in the crop response to variations in environmental conditions, especially light quality and quantity. During cloudy periods the EC of the nutrient solution can be raised by addition of potassium, provided by potassium sulfate. This will slow the vegetative growth of the plants. Further explanation of EC is given in *Questions No. 36 and 45.*

Tomatoes and cucumbers use a basic formulation having three levels. There are definite differences among formulae. Lettuce requires higher nitrogen, but lower potassium levels. A grower must start with basic formulations obtainable from the literature and then modify them into his "optimum" formulae, according to his experience with the crop under variations in the environment, especially sunlight hours and day length.

35. With my small hydroponic system very small amounts of micronutrients are very difficult to weigh accurately. Is there a method to make this easier?

If you have a small hydroponic system with a tank of less than 500 gallons, the amount of micronutrients required is very small. As a result, it is difficult to weigh on a triple beam balance that is capable of measuring to within one gram accurately. For example, the amount of ammonium molybdate needed for a 500-gallon tank to provide 0.03 ppm of molybdenum is 0.10 grams. This can only be weighed accurately on a very expensive electronic laboratory scale that could cost between $1500 and $2500.

You can avoid this problem by making up a concentrated stock solution at 400 times normal strength and storing it in a dark container. Make up enough micronutrients to last for several months. Do not include iron chelate, as it is required in an amount large enough to weigh with a triple beam balance. You can make the same concentration of all of the micronutrients (with the exception of iron), putting them all together in one dark container—after dissolving them separately. *We must work through an example to demonstrate the calculations.*

Assume that you have a 10-gallon stock storage container.

(1) Mo: 0.03 ppm (mg/l)
Source: ammonium molybdate
0.03 mg/l × 1.733 (reciprocal of fraction of Mo in ammonium molybdate) = 0.052 mg/l
That is, 1.733 mg of ammonium molybdate has 1 mg of Mo.

(2) Percent purity (95%):
100/95 × 0.052 mg/l = 0.055 mg/l

(3) For 10 U.S.-gallon stock tank:
37.85 l (liters) × 0.055 mg/l = 2.082 mg

(4) 400 × concentration:
400 × 2.082 = 832.8 mg or: 0.833 gm

Note: This is still a very small weight. It can be increased in several ways: (i) Use a larger stock tank (for example, 20 gallons); (ii) Increase the concentration to 600 × (still within solubility levels). *We shall use a larger storage tank.*

(5) For 20 U.S.-gallon stock tank: 2 × 2.082 mg = 4.16 mg

For 400 × concentration: 400 × 4.16 mg = 1664 mg or: 1.66 gm

This is now large enough to weigh. We still must do one more step, calculate the volume of this 400 × stock solution to be added to the 500-gallon nutrient tank to obtain a 1 × strength solution.

(6) Each gallon of stock solution has enough ammonium molybdate for 400 gallons of final 1 × strength solution. Therefore, for a 500-gallon tank we need: 500/400 × 1 gal = 1.25 gallons of stock solution. That is: 1.25 × 3.785 = 4.73 liters.

The same procedure must be used to calculate the amounts of the other components of the micronutrient stock solution. Since the stock solution will contain 400 times strength of all the micronutrients, the 4.73 liters to be added to the 500-gallon tank will provide the correct levels of all the micronutrients present in the stock solution. If our stock tank contains 20 gallons, it will last for: 20/1.25 = 16 changes (4 months). If this is too long (as precipitation may eventually form), do not be afraid to throw it out after several months; the total amount of nutrients used to make up the stock solution is very small.

36. A friend growing tomatoes told me that I must be careful when adjusting my nutrient solution that I keep the ratios of the various elements the same. What did he mean by this?

As you are aware, it is important to adjust the nutrient formulation according to changes in the environmental conditions, especially sunlight hours. It is necessary to increase the EC under cloudy conditions, with the addition of potassium sulfate. Also, you may use sodium or calcium chloride if no chloride or very low levels (less than 10 ppm) are present in the raw water. When adjusting these macroelement levels to raise the EC, they should be kept in the same ratios, with the exception of potassium, which may be raised. Various recommendations include a spring versus summer ratio of K:N of 1.4:1 to 1.8:1, respectively. Phosphorous is maintained between 40 and 50 ppm. A ratio of 1.5:1 of K:Ca is suggested throughout the crop by Dutch growers, with a ratio of Ca:Mg of 4:1 in the slab solution for the whole season. Be careful not to raise the ratio of N beyond optimum when you add calcium nitrate to obtain a higher calcium level. You will need to raise the potassium and magnesium levels, using the sulfate forms to keep these ratios the same.

37. My water is very hard. Is it suitable for hydroponics or must it be treated?

Hard water containing calcium and magnesium carbonates is normally suitable for growing plants. Both calcium and magnesium are macronutrients required by plants. Normal hard waters will not exceed the needed levels of these elements in a nutrient solution. Most nutrient solutions use 200 ppm of calcium and 50 to 60 ppm of magnesium. The amount of these elements in the raw water must be deducted from those called for in the nutrient formulation before calculating the weights of fertilizers used to provide the correct levels in the nutrient solution. In fact, the presence of calcium and magnesium in raw water can reduce the amount of fertilizers required in making up the nutrient solution.

The presence of low levels of carbonate in raw waters stabilizes the pH of the nutrient solution by resisting sudden drops in the pH. This is termed "buffering capacity." It is advisable to have 30 – 50 ppm of carbonate/bicarbonate level in your nutrient solution to reduce rapid shifts in pH. If your raw water is very pure, without any carbonates, it is recommended to add some potassium carbonate or bicarbonate to assist in stabilizing the pH of the nutrient solution.

The presence of sodium chloride in raw water is a different story. If levels of sodium chloride exceed 50 ppm, there may be potential problems in the growing of specific crops, depending upon their tolerance. Some herbs such as watercress and mint will tolerate higher levels of sodium chloride than do tomatoes or cucumbers. Also, if a closed hydroponic system is used, the level of sodium chloride will build up with the circulation of the solution past the plants. The plants will absorb water faster than the elements, thus reducing the volume of water, necessitating the addition of water as it circulates back to the nutrient tank. At the same time, as the plants do not assimilate the sodium chloride, the level will increase in the solution with the addition of water, eventually arriving at a concentration toxic to the plants. In this case, a water treatment facility using a process such as reverse osmosis must be installed to remove the sodium chloride.

38. I have heard that some bicarbonate in the raw water is good. What level is optimum and why?

Bicarbonate resists shifts in pH. The optimum level of bicarbonate to offer sufficient "buffering action" is between 20 and 40 ppm. If the bicarbonate content increases, the pH will rise. If too much acid is added to adjust the pH, too much of the bicarbonate is neutralized and the solution pH becomes unstable, resulting in large pH fluctuations. Maintain less that 100 ppm bicarbonate—maximum. Nitric acid is preferred to adjust the pH as it adds nitrogen. With low-bicarbonate raw water, D. H. Marlow (1993) suggests adding potassium bicarbonate at the rate of 2 grams of potassium bicarbonate per liter of water, which should cause a pH change of 1 unit.

39. My water comes from the city and is chlorinated. I can smell the chlorine; is this a problem for my crops?

The chlorine in the city water is added to kill bacteria. It does not create problems for your plants as it is highly volatile, and it evaporates from the water as soon as exposed to air. By the time your solution reaches the roots of the plants the chlorine will have dispersed. As you fill your nutrient tank, allowing the water to fall into the tank will aerate the water and at the same time allow the chlorine to escape from the water. But remember that chloride is different. It is toxic to plants at levels above 100 ppm. Most growers like to keep chloride levels below 50 ppm. Chloride is a microelement essential for plant growth and development. Plants need about 5 ppm of chloride.

Because many of the newer greenhouse grade fertilizers are fairly pure, chloride may not be present as an impurity. For this reason, it may be necessary to add some chloride in the form of calcium chloride if your raw water is very pure or if you use reverse osmosis treatment of the raw water.

40. My water is very hard so I had to install a reverse osmosis unit to remove all of the elements. Can the cost of operating this water treatment unit be reduced in any way?

To reduce the volume of treated water you may blend back some of your raw water. The percentage of blend-back water is dependent upon what elements are present in the raw water and the concentration. If the raw water is relatively low in sodium chloride, you may blend back a volume of water until your chloride levels reach about 10–15 ppm. Also, if the hydroponic system is a closed one, the level of chloride must be kept below 5–6 ppm or an accumulation of chloride may occur as the solution is recycled. Blending back raw water will also increase the bicarbonate level in the solution, which will stabilize the pH through its buffering action.

41. With my hard raw water can the high bicarbonate levels make it difficult to lower the pH? Can the bicarbonate level be so high as to cause nutritional deficiencies?

If the water is very basic due to high bicarbonate, it will require more acid to lower the pH. You can use a larger volume and/or a more concentrated solution of acid to lower the pH. The high bicarbonate will not prevent the lowering of the pH by addition of acid. With high bicarbonate levels the buffering action will stabilize the pH, slowing any change once it is adjusted. As long as the pH level is maintained at optimum levels for nutrient uptake by the plants, it will not cause nutritional deficiencies.

42. One of my stock tanks is depleted faster than the other. What might be the problem?

Check all of your water lines for filling the tank. It could be a leaking gate valve. Just dripping constantly will add sufficient volume of water to the tank to increase its volume. The other possibility is that one of your injector heads is out of adjustment. Calibrate the volume of each head according to the manufacturer's instructions. Each head must pump exactly the same volume (with the exception of the acid head) per stroke.

2,300-gallon stock tanks A & B for a large injector nutrient system. Courtesy of California Watercress, Inc., Fillmore, California.

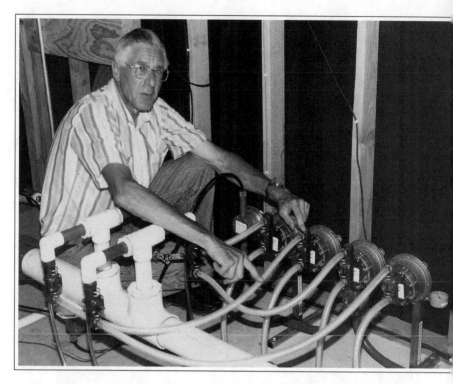

(See p. 39.) Calibration of injector heads is important so that they pump the correct volume of stock solution to obtain the exact ratio of stock solution to raw water. Each head must pump the same volume per stroke. Courtesy of California Watercress, Inc., Fillmore, California.

Tomatoes

Nutrition

43. I wish to grow tomatoes, cucumbers and peppers. What substrate is the best for these crops?

In general, vine crops, which have a relatively long cropping period—up to 10 months—require a medium rather than "water only" (as is NFT). Media which can be used for the crops you want are rice hulls, sawdust, rockwool and perlite. All are contained in bags, with a drip irrigation system feeding each plant individually. These substrates provide structure to maintain the roots at high oxygen levels. The substrate must not compact, as that will cause a lack of oxygenation and subsequent root death, reducing yields substantially.

Rockwool and perlite are the most readily available, as they can be shipped long distances due to their light weight. Rice hulls are specific to areas or countries having a lot of rice production. Sawdust culture is common in British Columbia, Canada, where a large lumber industry exists. A restraint on sawdust is that it must be from softwood trees such as Douglas fir and hemlock. Pine sawdust can be a problem with the high levels of turpines in the wood. However, if suitable sawdust is available it is usually much cheaper than rockwool or perlite. It must be bagged, as with the case of the other media.

44. With my tomato crop, the nutrient solution pH and EC does not change much over the weeks. I presently test the solution every day and would like to know whether I could save time and test it every other day or so since it is very stable?

You should be very happy that your solution maintains a stable pH and EC. However, this does not indicate that the solution need not be tested regularly. As the plants mature and produce fruit under varying sunlight conditions, the pH and EC of the solution may change greatly from one day to the next as nutrient assimilation rates change. It is recommended to test the pH and EC of the nutrient solution at least two to three times a day at different hours of the day. Always take samples in the greenhouse, selecting the slabs or growing bags to be tested at random. Take samples of the solution entering and leaving the growing medium to determine the uptake of nutrients. Record all readings for future reference to assist in making decisions on changes to be made in the formulation during changes in plant generative versus vegetative growth.

45. I have difficulty in judging whether my tomatoes are growing correctly to produce fruit or are too vegetative. What are the characteristics of a productive plant and how should the nutrient solution be adjusted to favor fruit production under cloudy conditions?

Here is a quick summary of generative versus vegetative plant characteristics. Generative tomato plants have dark-yellow flowers close to the top of the plant that open fast and uniformly within the truss. The top leaves of the plant are short, dark and firm. Truss stems are thick, sturdy, short and curved. Many fruit form quickly with good shape.

Vegetative plants have pale, light-yellow color and form far under the top of the plant. Flowers open poorly and sepals "stick" together. Leaves are open, flat, long, light-green and soft. Truss stems are thin, long and sticking upwards. Few fruits develop slowly and are small, with poor shape.

Under cloudy, poor light conditions the EC should be raised to slow vegetative growth. The EC of the substrate should be raised to between 3 and 6 mMho while the run-off should be between 2.5 and 4 mMho. Under poorer light conditions, raise the EC to the higher levels. As mentioned earlier, under *Questions No. 34* and *36,* raise the EC, by the addition of macroelements. Use potassium sulfate to raise the potassium ratio. Alternatively, calcium or sodium chloride may be used, provided the raw water is free of chloride. Do not raise the chloride level above 10-15 ppm. Other macroelements may be added as long as their ratios remain the same.

46. I understand that, in general, it is not necessary to adjust the micronutrient levels during plant growth. Under what conditions is it necessary to adjust these ratios?

In areas of high sunlight, such as the southwestern U.S., plants require more copper, iron, manganese and zinc as they are part of the photosynthesis pathways. Any changes made must be small, but they are necessary. Growers must monitor nutrient levels in both the solution and plant tissues. Relate these changes in uptake to plant growth and environmental conditions, especially day length and light intensity.

47. What is the best method of regulating feeding cycles to adjust EC of slabs in winter versus summer months?

During summer months with high light and low relative humidity conditions, plants have high transpiration. The EC of the slab will rise as water is taken up rapidly by the plants. In this case, it is best to reduce the duration of the cycles and increase the frequency of cycles per day. Also, lower the EC of the nutrient solution; that will prevent a rise of EC in the medium.

During low light and high relative humidity of winter months you need to increase the EC in the substrate to prevent vegetative growth. Increase the duration of feed cycles and reduce the frequency of cycles.

48. Will changing the percentage of leachate have any affect on generative versus vegetative phases of my plants? How should leachate be manipulated to bring about such changes?

The changing of percentage leachate will affect the growth of your plants. Over the 24-hour period during high light summer months you should leach at rates of 30 to 35 percent. During the most active growing period of the day, from 10:00 AM to 3:00 PM, additional leaching will lower the EC in the slab and provide additional water to compensate for the very high loss of water through transpiration (see *Question No. 47*). Under low light levels (cloudy days), less leaching will tend to raise the EC in the slab and favor generative growth.

49. Using my start tray, it irrigates the same duration of an irrigation cycle each time the cycle is activated, because the duration of the cycle is preset. How could it be made more responsive to what the plant needs during changing environmental conditions?

The start tray only initiates a watering cycle, it does not stop it. The cycle stops according to the predetermined time duration setting the grower has selected. To overcome this problem of being unresponsive to existing conditions it would be necessary to manually adjust the preset cycle duration for sunny versus cloudy days. The start tray tends to underwater on hot sunny days if operated on a time duration and will tend to overwater on cloudy days.

To achieve more optimum watering cycles, a combined control of time and solar input will regulate the cycles more responsively to plant needs. The solar input controlled through a computer provided with a weather station, could override the time setting.

50. When taking tissue analysis samples I am unsure of which tomato leaves should be used. Is there a standard procedure for this?

If your plants are suffering nutrient deficiency damage, take some samples within the damaged tissue, but not in the area of extreme browning (necrosis) if it covers a large part of the leaf. Use leaves showing some damage, generally a chlorotic (yellowing) of the tissue, but before they become so stressed to turn brown and dry.

If you are taking tissue samples to monitor the crop, always take the same area of the plant in order to get tests on a standard basis. Normally, use the end leaflet of the most recently mature leaf. Follow instructions from the laboratory to which you are submitting the sample for testing. For example, some laboratories say to use the fifth leaf down from the growing tip of the main stem and include both petiole and leaf blade. Take at least ten samples.

Always send a nutrient solution sample for testing at the same time in order to be able to relate the solution element levels to those of the tissue.

51. How should plant tissue leaves be prepared for sending to the laboratory? Some people tell me to dry the leaves in the microwave.

Never dry the leaves in the microwave as this will rupture the cells in the tissue, causing them to lose their liquid contents which contain many of the elements. Do not ship leaves in a plastic bag, as the lack of air will cause them to ferment. Lay the leaves out for one day, then put them in a brown paper bag for shipping. Most laboratories will provide these bags upon request.

52. I hear many opinions on the use of ammonium nitrogen. Some growers like to use a small amount while others do not use any. What guidelines would you suggest?

If you operate a greenhouse in the more northerly latitudes, it is best not to use ammonium forms of nitrogen during the late fall to early spring (October— April). During the high light periods, use no more than 10 percent of ammonium form of nitrogen. The other 90 percent of nitrogen should come from nitrates such as calcium and potassium nitrates. In high light areas of the Southwest you can use 10 percent ammonium nitrate most of the year as long as there is ample sunlight. During cloudy periods lasting several days discontinue its use.

53. Sometimes my tomatoes are "blocky" or "puffy," that is, the fruit is soft and somewhat square. What is causing this malformation of fruit?

This is caused by poor pollination. With low pollination, few seeds form in the locules (fruit sections), causing them to become flat. This poor pollination is due to too high or too low relative humidity during pollination (see *Question No. 104 and 137*). It can also be a result of low levels of potassium.

54. How can shelf life be increased in my tomatoes? The fruit becomes "mealy."

Potassium is responsible for helping tomatoes form firmly, providing long shelf life. Of course, other nutritional disorders, such as calcium deficiency, will give similar results, as cell walls lack the supporting element, calcium pectate.

Environmental Conditions and Plant Culture

55. I wish to grow tomatoes. When looking at various seed catalogs I find many varieties. What varieties are most suitable to greenhouse hydroponic culture?

In the greenhouse you must grow staking not bush varieties. Staking varieties are indeterminate, unlike the determinate bush varieties. That is, these varieties will continue to grow upwards and produce fruit as long as they are healthy. In a greenhouse there is ample vertical space, so it is advantageous to use plants that can grow very tall and continue producing over a period of nine to ten months.

For the controlled environment of a greenhouse, you must also select special greenhouse varieties, not field staking varieties. The most widely used varieties now come from Holland. Among other important factors in choosing a variety is the amount of sunlight in your area and the size of fruit your market demands. Some of the more popular varieties being used at present include: Bounty, Caruso, Laura, Belmondo, Match, Trend, Apollo, Blitz and Trust. Blitz needs lots of light, so under poor light it becomes very vegetative. Trend and Apollo do not form as large a fruit as do some of the others. The most popular variety at present is Trust, which has uniform fruit ripening and average fruit weight of 180-280 grams (6-10 ounces). The North American market generally likes the beefsteak larger fruit varieties.

56. Sometimes I encounter dry rockwool blocks or slabs. What is causing this lack of water retention?

Dry slabs or blocks result from insufficient watering or not soaking the rockwool long enough before using it. Rockwool should be soaked with the nutrient solution for one to two days prior to use. Blocks may be placed under a mist system or watered by hand. Placing the drip lines into the slabs, without cutting the drainage holes, soaks them adequately. Fill the slabs with nutrient solution, then check them for leaks. Irrigate the slabs several times a day to keep them full, using water of pH 5.0-5.2 (the slab pH is 7.0-8.5). After stabilizing the pH, use a solution of pH 5.5-6.0.

57. A friend told me that I should remove the wrapper on the rockwool blocks after transplanting my tomato seedlings into them. What effect would this have on my plants; would it increase root aeration?

Do not remove the wrappers on the rockwool blocks. They are on the blocks to prevent algae growth and to retain the structure of the blocks when set onto the slabs. Oxygenation would not be significantly improved with the removal of the wrapper. In addition, as the plants grow into the slab below upon transplanting, almost all of the roots will be in the slab not in the block. Any additional aeration in the blocks would have no beneficial effect.

58. I have heard the term "root pruning" and that it is important in the growing of healthy seedlings. What is it and how important is it in producing healthy plants?

Root pruning is a process for preventing roots from growing out of the seedling blocks. It is important that the plant roots do not accumulate at the bottom of the blocks, because when transplanting the roots will be damaged as they are being separated from neighboring blocks. This will create a lot of transplant "shock," and at the same time provides easy entry to plant pathogens.

If the seedlings are placed on a screen bench, or other well-aerated surface, the roots that grow out of the cubes will become desiccated. The larger root mass will continue growing within the blocks. Thus the roots will not be damaged upon transplanting, and the large internal mass of roots will quickly grow into the slab or other medium below. Transplant shock will be at a minimum, with their "taking hold" within a week.

59. I live in British Columbia, where the sunlight hours during the winter months is very low. Sometimes we receive less than 30 hours a month from November through January. How should I schedule my tomato crop and should I use artificial supplementary lighting?

Most growers in the more northerly latitudes use a single annual cropping system for tomatoes. Sow the seeds in mid-November for transplanting to larger rockwool blocks by late November. Keep the seedlings in one section of the greenhouse under HID (high intensity discharge) lighting with a minimum of 5,500 lux (510 foot candles) intensity at seedling height. By the first to second weeks of December, set the transplants on top of the rockwool slabs or other substrate bags, but do not place them in the slabs. This will allow the plants to continue growing slowly.

When the first flower buds appear, by early January, place the transplants into the slabs or bags for further rooting into the substrate. First harvest should occur by mid-February. The last harvest will take place about mid-November. During the sowing of seeds for the next crop, remove all the old plants and clean up the greenhouse.

While supplementary artificial lighting is beneficial for the seedlings, it is not economically feasible for the subsequent growing of the crop in the greenhouse. Supplementary lighting in the seedling area should be on for 14 to 18 hours per day. During sunny days, the lights could be turned off from about 11:00 AM until 2:00 PM but keep them on before and after that time to make up the 14- to 18-hour day.

60. I am confused as to what medium should be used to start my tomato seedlings. I wish to use perlite culture for the growing beds, so what would be the best way of growing the seedlings?

There are a number of ways to grow your seedlings that would be suitable for perlite culture. While cost may be a factor, the most important consideration is producing the very best quality plants. The substrate must have good drainage, yet not dry rapidly. Regardless of the seedling substrate, it is important to transplant to rockwool blocks as a second stage. Use the 3-inch (7.5-cm) rockwool blocks for tomatoes.

Sow the seeds in 1-inch rockwool cubes, granular rockwool placed in styrofoam trays of 240 cells or "Oasis Horticubes." All are sterile, but need to be thoroughly saturated to eliminate dry spots. Purchase rockwool blocks with the large holes so that these rockwool cubes will fit inside. Transplant the seedlings to the rockwool blocks after the first true leaves unfold and the second set are visible (after about 14 days).

61. I am uncertain whether I should use nutrient solution or raw water on my seedlings, please advise.

It is best to use raw water during the germination of the seed. As the seeds germinate and the cotyledons unfold, continue using water only. Once the first set of true leaves begin to open, use a dilute nutrient formulation of about one-third strength. The seedlings may be irrigated by overhead sprinklers or by hand. It is important to adjust the amount of water applied according to weather conditions. Too much or too little water will be detrimental to seed germination. Whenever watering, water sufficiently to obtain adequate leaching to prevent any salt buildup.

62. Some growers tell me to cover the tomato seed in the cubes. Is this important?

As you are aware, the rockwool and Oasis cubes come with small holes in them for placing the seed. Placing coarse vermiculite over the holes on top of the seed will assist the shedding of the seed coats. However, be careful not to use peat or fine vermiculite or perlite; it will reduce oxygenation of the seed. Oxygen is critical to seed germination, as it is required in the respiration processes of the seeds for the growth of the embryo. Perlite can cause problems with algae growth. Covering the seed will help to prevent any possible desiccation during germination should you fail to water in time.

Sometimes growers wish to cover the cubes with polyethylene. This poses two problems, especially for larger seeds that require more oxygen, as they quickly convert starch in the cotyledons to sugar in their germination. The polyethylene cover will reduce oxygen entering the seeds. At the same time, heat buildup under the polyethylene can raise temperatures above optimum levels for seed germination.

Overall, if you are willing to spend the time in closely watching the watering of the seed it would not be necessary to cover the seed.

63. When sowing my tomato seeds, how much extra seed should I sow to compensate for those that do not germinate?

To determine this look at the percentage viability on the seed package. If the seed company indicates a seed germination test of 95 percent, you need to sow an extra 5 percent to compensate for this loss. In addition, look at the age of the seed and when its germination was tested. The older the seed, the lower will be its viability. Store seed in your refrigerator, but not in the freezer. Tomato seeds will last for several years, unlike lettuce seed which losses its viability substantially within four to five months, even under refrigeration.

You must also consider several other factors. If you are in an area of poor sunlight during the season of germinating the seeds, expect poorer germination and more variability in the vigor of the seedlings. There will always be some poor plants as a result of slow germination. Plants that germinate late tend to be smaller and weaker than those which germinate very rapidly. Any such "sickly" looking plants should not be used. Follow the general rule, "If you go in with poor plants expect poor production from those plants."

In summary, sow an additional 8 to 10 percent above the number adjusted for after taking into consideration the germination percentage. Therefore, if the seed is 95 percent viable, oversow between 13 to 15 percent.

64. I am growing my tomato seedlings under artificial lighting. What photoperiod should I use?

Using an 18-hour photoperiod will keep the seedlings short and stalky.

65. What are the optimum temperatures for the germination of tomato seeds?

Medium temperature should be maintained between 77 and 79 F (25-26 C) for four to five days during germination. Do not exceed 83-84 F (29 C).

66. My tomato plants often get "leggy"; why is this?

There are a number of reasons for your plants becoming leggy (tall and thin). One of the main reasons is lack of light. When beginning tomato seedlings in November or December under short days and low light conditions, especially in more northerly latitudes, supplementary artificial lighting must be used, as outlined in *Question No. 59.* Adequate spacing of the plants is also important, to allow light to penetrate the canopy.

Transplant the seedlings into the 3-inch blocks as soon as the first true leaves open and the second set is visible (12-14 days after sowing). If the plants are a little leggy, transplant them into the blocks by turning them 180 degrees and bending the shoots up, with the leaves pointing upward. The plants will form adventitious roots along the stems covered in the blocks. Space the blocks in a checkerboard pattern that will give a 6-inch (15-cm) spacing between plants. This will be sufficient spacing to grow the transplants to about five weeks from sowing. After that, they need to be placed on the slabs or bags in the production area, as described in *Question No. 59.*

Other environmental factors as well as the nutrient formulation are important in keeping the seedlings sturdy and somewhat hardened. Enrich with about 1000 ppm of carbon dioxide. Keep temperatures a little lower to harden the plants, at between 64 and 68 F (18 – 19 C). Water less frequently, allowing the plants to undergo slight stress, but do not allow them to wilt. The EC could be raised by addition of potassium sulfate, but remember that during this seedling stage, a one-third concentration of the formulation is being used, so the EC should be about 1.5 to 2 mMho.

67. What are the correct temperature regimes for tomatoes during their early growth stages?

The day temperature for the post-germination period of days 5 to 12 from seeding should be 73 F (23 C); night temperature should be 68 F (17 C). During the first transplant into rockwool blocks keep temperatures at 68 F (20 C) day and 63 F (17 C) at night.

68. Some growers have told me that if I rub the tomato seedlings this will make their stems become thicker, is that true and if so how should it be done?

Research has shown that wind action activates a hormone in the seedlings, which thickens the stems. Wind action in the greenhouse may be created with the use of blowers in the seedling area or by passing a piece of foam rubber mat back and forth over the seedlings for one minute per day over a three-week period. This will produce plants with shorter, thicker stems, which will encounter less stress during transplanting, resulting in more productive plants.

69. What precautions should be taken when transplanting my tomato seedlings to the grow bags or slabs?

First, water the seedlings well before removing them from the seedling area. This will prevent them from wilting when they are uprooted and placed upon the grow bags or slabs. The best time to transplant is in the late afternoon so that they can adjust overnight to the conditions on the bags or slabs. Alternatively, transplant on cloudy days. However, in more northerly areas the sunlight during December, when transplanting, is very weak, so excessive light should not be a problem. Remember that in the seedling area the plants were very closely spaced so they retained more moisture. As they are separated after transplanting, they will lose more moisture with the increased air exchange.

As mentioned in *Question No. 58,* if the seedlings are set on open benches, allowing good root pruning, there will be less wilting and transplant shock, due to less root damage in removing them. It is also recommended to drench the seedlings with a beneficial microorganism such as "Mycostop" prior to transplanting, to prevent infection of the seedling by *Fusarium* and *Pythium* root rot fungi.

Sterilize all wagons, trays, etc. to be used in transporting the seedlings, prior to using them. This will eliminate infectious fungal spores from contact with the roots of the seedlings when being transported. Disinfect with a 10 percent bleach solution. When moving the transplants, keep them in the trays until placing them directly onto the growing bags or slabs.

70. When placing the tomato transplants onto the slabs beside the hole, what level of EC is recommended during winter days?

For northerly regions it is best not to set the transplants into the holes of the slabs until the first truss has been pollinated and the flowers of the second are visible. Set the plants on top of the slab next to the hole, not allowing the roots to enter the slab. The EC of the block should be 4.0 mMho and the EC of the slab about 3.5 mMho.

71. When should the tomato plants be strung to support them?

Support the plants with the overhead strings at the time of transplanting. They must not be allowed to fall over as they continue growing, as that will damage their stems. All the strings should be in place before transplanting. This is part of the clean up, the preparation of the greenhouse while the seedlings are growing in the seedling house or area.

After transplanting, attach the string to the base of the plant, on the stem immediately under a sturdy leaf petiole, with a plastic plant clip. Do not place the plant clip under a cotyledon, or the first true leaf, if it is weak. You can also wrap the string around the plant stem, upward, several times, in a clockwise direction, to give it further support.

72. I am preparing my greenhouse for transplanting and would like to know the best method of putting up the support strings, what length and what type of string to use.

Use plastic white twine for supporting the plants. The string is tied to overhead cables. Secure the string on the cables at gutter height directly above the plant location. Depending upon the length of your cropping period, you must leave adequate additional string at the cable level to allow for lowering of the plants as they grow. Keep at least 15 to 20 feet (4.5 - 6m) extra for lowering the plants, if you are using a single annual crop. The most widely used method employs "tomahooks" to secure the twine and plants to the overhead cables. The twine is wound around the hook and is easily unwound for later lowering of the plants. The hook can be slid along the cable to move the plants as they are being lowered. These "tomahooks" are available 10 and 15 cents each, depending on quantity purchased.

73. As my tomato plants continue growing upward, at what intervals should I place vine clips for support on the twine?

Tomato plants need adequate support so that they will not fall under heavy fruit load. Place vine clips about every foot (30 cm). Be sure that they are located under strong leaf petioles and securely affixed to the twine. As the plants are lowered, as they grow, you may remove some of the lower clips. For later reuse, soak them with 10 percent solution of bleach (sodium hypochlorite) for about 30 minutes, rinse and dry them. Vine clips should be placed on the plants at least once a week to keep up with their growth. Generally, they are put on the plants while removing the suckers.

74. I have been removing the suckers of my tomatoes with pruning shears. Is this the correct way, and when should they be removed?

The axillary shoots that grow between the main stem and the leaf petioles must be removed to maintain a single stem plant. They must be removed at an early stage when they are about 1-1.5 inches (2-3cm) long. If they are removed late, food reserves will be lost and the plant will become more vegetative.

Do not cut the suckers with pruning shears, unless you have neglected removing them and they have become too large to snap off by hand. Snap off the suckers by placing your thumb and forefinger of one hand on the main stem directly below the sucker's base and grasp the sucker with the thumb and forefinger of the other hand giving a rapid jerk to break it clean. To prevent the tomato acid from sticking to your hands, you may wear disposable surgeon's gloves.

75. I have noticed that some of my tomato plants stop growing even though they are indeterminate. As they no longer produce fruit what should I do with them?

Sometimes tomato plants will not form a growing point as they mature. This will terminate their production unless you allow one of the suckers below to take over. These "blind" plants are common, so the grower should always look at the tip of the plant when removing the suckers. If a plant does not have a distinct growing tip, be sure to let one of the lower side shoots continue to grow and become the principal stem. It may be a good idea to place a flag of colored tape on the string of these plants, as a reminder, so the developing sucker is not inadvertently removed.

76. When working with my tomato plants, I have found some plants that bifurcate, forming two growing tips. Should one be removed and if so which one?

Tomato plants often form two growing tips. One should be removed. You may pinch the tip of the one you wish to terminate; or, if it is very large, cut it off with pruning shears. In general, leave the healthiest stem to grow. Usually you can see which is the principal stem by looking at the location of the flower cluster. Bifurcation often takes place close to the flower cluster. The main stem will be the shoot that contains the lower flower cluster.

Axillary shoots must be removed early to maintain a single stem.

77. Sometimes a plant is broken, or a plant has to be removed due to disease. What can be done to compensate for this loss of production?

If a plant is broken, look for a possible second sucker forming in one of the lower leaf axes and allow it to grow into a new principal stem. Failing this, or if the loss of a plant is due to disease, permit one of the suckers of the neighboring plant to grow and train it into the empty space left after removal of the diseased plant. This can be done as long as the adjacent plant is healthy.

It is very important to handle the plants carefully to avoid breaking stems. Breaking of plant stems becomes more prevalent when the plants must be lowered as they grow upward toward their overhead supports. The plants become more brittle at their base with age.

78. I have noticed a lot of plants in my crop having large leaves and thick stems. What causes this?

These plants are termed "bullish" when they have large stems and leaves with long clusters and flowers not opening properly (the sepals "stick together"). This is an indication that the plants are very vegetative and must be shifted into a more generative state by changing the environment and nutrient formulation as discussed in *Questions No. 36, 45, 94, 98* and *100*. Plants in a vegetative phase of growth will result in a substantial loss of fruit production.

79. As lower leaves of my tomato plants turn yellow and need to be removed, how often should they be removed and how many is it advisable to remove per week?

As the lower leaves yellow they should be removed to provide better air movement at the base of the plant, as pointed out in *Questions No. 95* and *96*. Snap these leaves off by hand up to the present bearing truss. As a rule, do not remove more than three to four leaves per week. Do not remove green leaves, as they will still provide food to the plant.

While some growers let the removed leaves dry in the aisles without removing them, I like to remove all debris immediately to prevent any possible spread of diseases or any invitation for animals such as mice to enter the greenhouse. This also applies to any damaged fruit that has been removed. If you do not take it out of the greenhouse immediately you are going to encounter unwanted problems. A secondary note to this is that in areas where there are snakes, especially rattlesnakes, you will be inviting them into your house, as they will go after the mice and even you!

80. I am uncertain as to how much I should prune the flower clusters and when. Is it sometimes better to allow more fruit to form than other times?

In general, flower clusters should be pruned to form four to five fruit each. Prune them when the fruit has set and formed to a pea size. At that time you will better be able to distinguish the healthiest fruit which will develop rapidly. Watch for any malformed fruit, those with blossom scars, other marks or bruises, etc. Remove these first. Ideally, the fruit should form starting at the back of the truss near the stem of the plant and progress uniformly outward. If a fruit is smaller, and yet nearer the stem, behind those forming outward from it, this fruit probably will not size well as the others compete with it for food; therefore, remove it.

Prune flower clusters when the fruit has set and formed to pea size. Note the receptive flowers with their petals bent backwards.

If your plants are vegetative, you may allow more fruit to form on some trusses to shift the plant into a generative state. On the contrary, if your plants are overloaded with fruit and the plant is off color, with thinning stems, you could reduce the number of fruit per truss for some time until the plant regains its vigor.

81. I find that some of the trusses of my plants break off under their heavy fruit load. What can be done to prevent this?

This can be particularly severe on the first four to five trusses of the plants. When pruning your clusters, place truss support clips on the stem of the cluster. Two types of plastic supports are available, a hook and an arch. One end of the truss hook is placed on the truss, with the hook on the other end attached to the stem of the plant, above a leaf petiole. These hooks keep the trusses from kinking and cutting off nutrient flow to the developing fruit. The truss arch is applied at an early stage when small fruits are forming. It is snapped onto the young truss stem, giving it enough support so as not to kink. The truss hooks may be used at a later stage as the fruit sizes. However, be careful not to allow the trusses to kink prior to using the supports, as a lot of damage will already have been done.

A recent suggestion has been made that cluster strength can be improved by injuring the cluster stem slightly. This is said to strengthen the stem connection so that support clips are not needed. Try if you are so inclined.

82. I get a lot of opinions on the correct spacing of tomato plants. Are there standard spacing dimensions; and what are the ranges under different light conditions?

Suggested spacing, on an area basis of the greenhouse, ranges from 3.5 to 4.3 square feet (0.3 to 0.4 square meters) per plant. (On a large scale, this is a population of 12,000 to 10,000 plants per acre or 31,000 to 25,000 plants per hectare.) Normal spacing is 3.5 square feet (0.3 square meters) per plant. (That is equivalent to 12,000 plants per acre.) Higher populations may be planted in areas of high sunlight, such as the southwestern United States and Mexico.

Plants are spaced in double rows, 20 to 25 inches (50 to 65 cm) apart, and 18 to 20 inches (45 to 50 cm) within each row. Aisles should be about 40 inches (1 m) wide between each set of double rows. (This spacing will fit 10,000 plants per acre with the aisle and a central passageway for access.)

Alternatively, when using rockwool culture, instead of forming double rows of plants, a single row of wide slabs, each supporting five plants, is used. The spacing between these single rows would be about 62 to 65 inches (157 to 165 cm). The plants are still trained into double rows, using the V-cordon pattern with the support strings, resulting in the same plant density as with the double row method.

83. I have heard of some growers planting fewer plants and, later, allowing one side shoot of each plant to grow in order to obtain the normal plant density. What are the procedures for that?

This has been done by a number of growers in the more northerly latitudes to overcome poor light conditions during the late winter to early spring months. This method can be used with rockwool, sawdust or perlite bags. Plants are spaced 30 inches (75 cm) within rows, with 18 to 20 inches (45-50 cm) between rows. This is equivalent to 6 square feet (0.6 square meters) per plant when the aisle width is taken into consideration.

This area is reduced to the normal 3.0-3.5 square feet (0.3-0.35 square meter) density by mid-April, when light has improved, by the following method.

Systematically increasing numbers of plants, about one sixth of them at a time, are allowed to bifurcate into two stems, with the growth of one side shoot, starting by the end of February. By the end of April, every plant has two stems; thus, the plant density is doubled. Of course, to be successful with this method of training you must have very healthy plants. There is more risk in loss of plants through diseases, as any one plant lost is equivalent to a production loss of two. The two principal stems must be trained as if they were individual plants, in terms of suckering and support. I think that experienced growers could use this method, but with care.

84. When my taller plants are lowered, the stems rest on top of the grow bags and the stems often develop fungal infection (Botrytis or gray mold); what can be done to prevent this problem?

This can easily be prevented by supporting the plant stems above the grow bags with wire hoops placed across the bags or slabs at the location of every plant. These hoops can be made of galvanized #8 or #9 wire. They should be wide enough to span the double row of plants and tall enough so that they support the stems about one foot (30 cm) above the floor. They will need to be pushed into the floor about four to six inches (10–15 cm) to remain in place. They also need to have a hairpin-shaped bend on the outer edges to keep the plant stems from falling over the outside edges. These wire hoops should be available commercially from greenhouse suppliers.

Supporting the plant stems above the slabs or bags will permit good ventilation at the base of the plants and maintain the stems dry, thus preventing *Botrytis* infection.

85. My neighbor grows tomatoes in his hydroponic greenhouse. He tells me that he has bumblebees in his house which pollinate the plants without his having to worry about it. How often should tomatoes be pollinated and what methods can be used?

Tomatoes are normally wind-pollinated, but in a greenhouse there is insufficient air movement to pollinate. It is very important to get the first flower trusses set in order to shift the plant into a generative state. Pollination can be done by hand, using a vibrator; in fact, that used to be the usual method. The vibrator is held lightly against the flower truss for several seconds, releasing the pollen from the flowers. This was done between 11:00 AM and 3:00 PM at least every other day, as flowers remain receptive about two days.

Even if you have a bee hive for flower pollination, it is necessary to visually check the pollination for effectiveness. It also does not hurt to pollinate the first several clusters using a vibrator, to ensure adequate pollination. Bumble bees are now a generally accepted method of pollination as they are effective and save a lot of labor. Fruit set will be visible as pea-sized fruit form within a week of pollination.

86. I find that some of my flowers are badly bruised by the bumblebees when pollinating. Is this a general problem and if so what should be done?

Bruising of the flower corolla (tube-like part of the flower) needs to be closely monitored. Flowers generally show between 90 and 100 percent bruising, but they should not have extreme damage, where the whole corolla browns. Too much damage to the flowers will cause fruit damage. Overworking of flowers may be due to too high a bee population or too few flowers opening at a given time, especially during cloudy, dark weather. Keep in mind that the population of one hive is sufficient to pollinate one-half acre (0.2 hectare) of tomatoes. The bees will survive an average of three to four months and hives cost about $350 each.

Under cloudy conditions, it is possible to reduce the activity of bees in working the flowers by placing a dish of bee pollen on top of the hive. But as soon as light conditions improve and flowers open, remove the pollen or the bees may become lazy and not work the flowers.

87. What does a receptive flower look like?

Flowers are receptive when their petals fold backwards. They will be fully open and have a nice, deep-yellow color. As mentioned earlier (*Question No. 45*), if flowers are light yellow or the sepals stick together, not allowing them to open, this indicates that the plants are too vegetative and must be shifted to a more generative state. Flowers remain receptive for about two days, so must be pollinated within that time. To check whether the pollen is flowing, simply hold a piece of black paper behind the flower while vibrating it with your fingers. The flowing pollen will be visible as it falls from the flower.

88. In the early morning I often notice water droplets along the edges of the leaves of my plants. What is this and is it indicative of a problem with my environmental control?

This is termed guttation, when plants have a high root uptake of water but cannot transpire fast enough to use all of the water taken up. The water "sweats" from special cells on the perimeter of the leaves. It can be common with European cucumbers that have a very large leaf area. It occurs in the early morning with high relative humidity levels. Relative humidity levels need to be monitored and automatically controlled by ventilation of the greenhouse. Guttation can favor fungal infection by providing high moisture on the leaves.

89. What is the optimum relative humidity for the growing of my tomato crop?

The optimum range of relative humidity in the greenhouse environment for tomatoes is between 70 percent and 80 percent. The relative humidity should be kept within this range day and night. It must be monitored and may be controlled automatically through ventilation of the greenhouse.

90. How do non-optimum levels of relative humidity affect tomatoes?

The shelf life of tomato fruit decreases as the relative humidity rises above optimum levels. High relative humidity causes clumping of the pollen in the flowers of tomatoes and thus causes misshapen fruit and poor pollination. Fruit set may be decreased. Low relative humidity can cause the pollen to dry and become infertile, resulting in poor fruit set.

91. High relative humidity and high temperatures result in low water deficit; what effect has this on my tomato plants?

If plants have a low water deficit, they will not take up water readily. The plants need to have a moisture deficit to make them work and remain generative (producing fruit). The water deficit will increase from morning to noon under increasing light and temperatures. As fans operate, producing good ventilation, the water deficit will increase, helping plants to increase water uptake through increased evapotranspiration. This rapid water uptake assists nutrient uptake to support rapid photosynthesis.

92. Under cloudy conditions I often notice that the greenhouse temperature rises and it is very moist. Will this reduce productivity of the tomatoes?

High temperatures combined with low light and high relative humidity will definitely reduce productivity. Under such conditions there is a net loss of food reserves, as high respiration, caused by high temperatures and low photosynthesis due to low light, do not allow the plant to produce sufficient photosynthates. High respiration causes stored food as starches to convert to sugars for energy used in the respiration processes. This causes vegetative growth instead of fruit growth. Under these high temperatures, the plants will expend energy trying to cool themselves. This is a further shift of food reserves away from fruit formation. If respiration is greater than photosynthesis, fruit loss will occur, especially at the fourth and fifth clusters.

At the same time, high relative humidity creates an ideal environment for fungal spore germination and subsequent disease infection.

The relative humidity and temperature may be lowered by ventilation. Even if it is raining outside, the relative humidity can be lowered in the greenhouse through ventilation. Fan-jets should operate steadily, with the shutters open. Overhead louvers can be opened in natural ventilation greenhouses to permit circulation of the air and its escape. As the moist outside air enters the greenhouse and its temperature is raised to that of optimum levels within the greenhouse, the relative humidity will fall. The relative humidity is a measure of the amount of moisture in the air. As air temperature is increased, the air is capable of holding more moisture. If the temperature of cool air of 100 percent relative humidity (RH) is raised as it enters the greenhouse, the RH in this air decreases. As it is mixed with the greenhouse air, it will reduce the overall RH in the house. Of course, in a hot tropical climate with high temperatures outside combined with high RH, the cooling capacity and reduction of moisture in the greenhouse is diminished.

93. During the summer, after a period of cloudy days, my tomato plants wilt during subsequent days of full sunlight. Should I shade during these sunlight days and by how much?

Shading for a few days, and only during the high light time of the day, will help. D. H. Marlow (1993) suggests the following procedure for acclimatization. During a sunny period, shade for the first three days only. As a guide, from 10:30 AM to 3:00 PM the first day, 11:30 AM to 2:00 PM the second day and on the third day from 12:00 noon to 2:00 PM.

94. To keep my tomato plants generative, how much difference should there be between night and day temperatures?

Generally, night temperatures should be 4 to 7 F (2-4 C) lower than day temperatures. If night temperatures are too high, respiration increases, causing conversion of starch to sugars and more vegetative growth.

The greenhouse should automatically control night temperatures through ventilation. If the temperature is too high, the plant must respire faster, and energy of the plant is lost in cooling itself.

95. I have noticed a lot of the lower leaves of the tomato plants yellowing. What causes this?

Leaves yellow as the plant produces ethylene. This may be caused by several factors. An oxygen deficit of the greenhouse air due to insufficient ventilation. Lack of light reaching the lower leaves. Unit heaters not having adequate ventilation. If the level of oxygen in the air falls below 19.5 percent, insufficient oxygen is present for complete combustion. There is always some senescence (yellowing) of lower leaves as the fruit ripens upward on the plant. These leaves should be removed as they senesce to provide better ventilation.

96. How should the yellow leaves on my tomato plants be removed and when?

As the lower leaves yellow below the clusters of fruit that have been harvested, they must be removed. They will have a natural abscission zone near the plant stem. This is a crack which develops in the plant trying to shed the leaf. Break the leaves of tomato plants by hand. Do not cut them—the abscission layer develops to seal off the exposed tissue from disease invasion. Removal of these leaves will be helpful when you lower the plant stems as the plant height increases, and will also provide more air movement around the base of the plant, reducing the relative humidity in that area of the plant. You should keep at least 5-6 feet (1.5-2 m) of good leaf growth on the upper part of the plant.

97. I have noticed that my tomato plants are darker green at midday than during the early morning. What is the problem?

This is actually an indication of the plants being in good generative state. During the early morning, the plants' water uptake will be equal to their loss through evapotranspiration. As the day progresses higher light intensity will cause the evapotranspiration rate to slightly exceed the water uptake, giving the plant a little stress, resulting in better fruiting.

98. My tomato plants have very thick stems and the upper leaves are coiled (spring-like shape). What has happened to them?

This is an obvious symptom of excess nitrogen, especially under cloudy/low light levels. The plants are too vegetative and must be shifted to a more generative state. Increasing the EC, as pointed out in *Questions No. 36* and *45,* can do this. Also, reduce the nitrogen level. One way is to eliminate the use of ammonium in the form of ammonium nitrate.

99. My tomato plants already have nine clusters as the first fruit is ripening. Is this late in the plant's stage of growth to begin producing ripe fruit?

Yes. It is very late for the plants to begin ripe fruit production. This indicates that the plants are too vegetative. You must shift them into a more generative state by using methods as discussed above in *Questions No. 36, 45, 91, 92* and *94*. When plants are properly balanced between fruiting and vegetative phases, fruit should ripen as the seventh flower cluster opens. If later, the plants are too vegetative. Flower color should be dark yellow, not light.

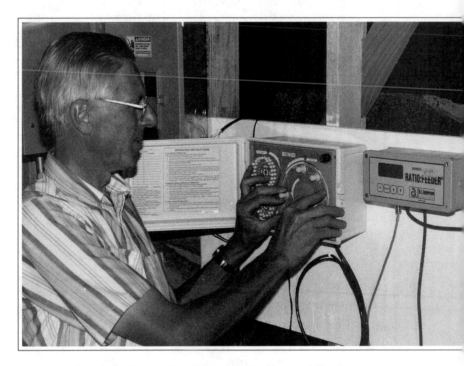

Adjust irrigation cycles on your controller to shift plants to a more generative state. Controllers should have a weekly clock (on the left), a 24-hr. clock (upper left) and an hourly cycle in minute gradations for each station (on the right). This is a 7-station controller. The controller must also have the capacity to initiate at least 24 cycles per day.

100. What are some other methods of shifting my plants from vegetative to generative state?

Here are a number of environmental and feeding adjustments that can be carried out to shift plants to a more generative state. Raise the humidity deficit by reducing the relative humidity through ventilation. Add carbon dioxide enrichment up to 1000 ppm. Raise the electrical conductivity of the nutrient solution. Make the irrigation cycle length longer, with less frequency. Start the irrigation cycles later in the morning, allowing slight water stress. Stop the irrigation cycles earlier in the late afternoon to early evening while the sun is still out. Prune trusses less, allowing more fruit per truss (from 5 to 6). Cool the temperatures faster in changing from day to night regime. Make the day-night temperature differential greater (up to 5 C or 9 F).

101. The undersides of the lower leaves of my tomato seedlings are purple. What is the problem?

This is not a problem; in fact, it indicates that the plants are a little "hard." They are storing starch. They will be strong and sturdy when transplanted. Good quality tomato transplants should be as wide as they are high. Keep temperatures of seedlings between 62 and 65 F (16.5-18 C). These cooler temperatures will help them to continue storing starch.

102. Many organic gardeners tell me that the tomatoes need vitamins, added to the nutrient solution. Is this true?

There is no physiological support indicating that vitamins are essential for plant growth. Do not confuse this with the fact that the plants manufacture their own vitamins during the processes of photosynthesis and respiration, utilizing essential elements present in the nutrient solution. According to principles of nutrient uptake by plant roots, large molecules, such as vitamins, are not able to pass through the root membranes. Uptake of minerals by plants is an electrochemical process very specific to the ions being transported from one side to the other of the cell membranes. Large organic compounds cannot be transported in this way, from the external environment to the plant's inner processes.

There is a specific relationship between ions and their carriers that transport them across cell membranes to enter the cell. Of course, organic molecules may be decomposed in the soil solution into their individual elements, which in their ionic state can be absorbed by the plant, providing they are required by the plant.

103. Some people tell me not to spend a lot of time in the greenhouse at night as the carbon dioxide levels may be harmful to one's health. Is that possible?

During the night, the plants are respiring, producing carbon dioxide as a by-product. If you remain in the greenhouse for many hours at night, you may find that you are tired from lack of optimum oxygen levels. This would be more noticeable if no ventilation is occurring in the greenhouse. Normally, people do not work in the greenhouse for a long period of time at night. People may be working at night in a packing facility associated with a greenhouse, but that would be separate from the greenhouse growing area, having its own environmental control.

104. I notice that under cloudy days my tomato flowers do not open well. What environmental conditions should be monitored and adjusted for producing receptive flowers?

All of the environmental conditions favorable to generative growth, as mentioned earlier (*Questions No. 89, 92, 94,* and *100*), contribute to good flower formation. Greenhouse temperatures should not fall below 60 F (15 C) at night or exceed 85 F (29 C) during the day. At higher or lower than optimum temperatures, pollen germination and pollen tube growth are reduced. This will slow fruit development.

It is important to keep relative humidity between 70 and 80 percent. Lower levels can desiccate the pollen while higher levels cause pollen to clump and stick. This lessens the movement of pollen from anthers to stigma, causing insufficient pollination for rapid fruit development and sizing of fruit.

105. In the past year I have seen a lot of tomatoes at the supermarket which are sold on their clusters. What are the advantages and disadvantages of growing these tomatoes; and are they special varieties?

When tomatoes are sold attached to their trusses they are called cluster (truss) tomatoes or tomatoes-on-the-vine (TOV). The entire cluster of tomatoes must be harvested at the same time with the fruit remaining on the cluster. The fruit must ripen uniformly and rapidly at the same time for good taste. This requires even pollination and fruit formation. The calyx must remain green during its shelf-life. Increased potassium levels, especially in the spring, will help.

There are red, orange and yellow varieties. All cluster tomatoes are of specific varieties such as Ambiance, Balance and Tradiro. It is important that the tomatoes are relatively large in size, have a red uniform color, fresh calyx and are firm for shipping. Tradiro is one the most common varieties grown, as it larger than some of the other varieties, with an average fruit weight between 120 and 150 grams (four to five ounces). It has vigorous growth and produces firm, red fruit. Good quality trusses should have between five and seven fruit.

Problems associated with cluster tomatoes include the fact that they are more labor intensive than single fruit, both in harvesting and handling. They should be harvested carefully and packed in the greenhouse to avoid having the fruit come off of the cluster. When on the supermarket shelf, if consumers handle them a lot they will separate from the cluster. This results in loss of product. To avoid this it is possible that the clusters could be packed in small, netted sacks similar to those used with carrots and onions. Another problem is that the production of cluster tomatoes is 15-20 percent less than that of the normal beefsteak varieties. Firmness of the fruit can also be a problem, especially if all the fruit of the cluster does not develop uniformly and ripen rapidly. The greatest advantage of cluster fruit is the higher price received for the product.

Cluster tomatoes now represent more than 10 percent of the total North American greenhouse production.

106. I am very confused as to when should my tomatoes be picked. What is a "ripe" tomato; and at what stage of color should it be harvested?

A true vine-ripened tomato should be picked when it is red. However, due to perishability they cannot be harvested in that state and shipped any distance. They can be harvested red for on-farm fruit stand sales. The state of color at harvesting is a function of the distance and time in shipping. The California Tomato Board publishes a chart on ripening stages of tomatoes. This is very helpful and may be obtained from them at the following address: 2017 N. Gateway, Suite 102, Fresno, CA 93727 or phone: (800) 827-0628.

For shipping, tomatoes should be picked at the "vine ripe" state defined as stages 2 to 3, with some varieties at stage 4 of this chart. Stage 2 is termed "breakers" when there is a definite break in color from green to yellow, pink or red on not more than 10 percent of the fruit surface. Stage 3 is "turning" when more than 10 percent but less than 30 percent of the surface shows this change in color. Stage 4 is "pink" when between 30 and 60 percent of the surface shows pink or red color. Stages 5 and 6, which are "light red" (60-90 percent pink to red surface) and "red" (more than 90 percent of surface is red), are suitable stages for harvesting for local markets and roadside fruit stands.

Remember that there are varietal differences in the firmness of tomatoes, their shipping ability and shelf-life, which will also influence the best time to harvest. For taste, of course, the more red the fruit the better will be its flavor, as long as it remains firm.

107. I produce lettuce and tomatoes. Can they be shipped together at the same temperatures?

For a short distance to local markets they probably could be shipped together, but you will have to compromise on the temperature. In refrigerating the lettuce, avoid chilling the tomatoes. Lettuce should be refrigerated at between 34 and 36 F (1-2.5 C); whereas, tomatoes should be shipped at temperatures between 55 and 60 F (13-16 C). Tomatoes, like tropical fruits, are susceptible to chilling injury when transported or stored at lower than recommended temperatures. Injured product may show discoloration and water-soaked areas, and have poor shelf life. The exposure period is very important in causing injury. For long distance shipping, it is best to ship tomatoes with other vegetables requiring the same temperature regimes—or ship them separately.

Both lettuce and tomatoes are highly sensitive to ethylene. They should not be shipped with other ethylene-producing fruits and vegetables such as apples, peaches or pears, as the ethylene produced by these fruits will cause premature ripening and will damage them.

In shipping or storage of tomatoes maintain relative humidity between 85 and 95 percent. The optimum relative humidity for lettuce is between 98 and 100 percent.

108. How often should I harvest my tomatoes; and what is the best way of picking them?

The tomatoes should be harvested every day so that they may be picked at the correct stage for shipping. If the greenhouse is less than half an acre (0.2 hectare) you probably can pick every other day. Pick in the late morning to early afternoon or in the late afternoon. The tomatoes must be picked when the fruit is dry. In the early morning, higher relative humidity may cause fruit to be moist. Also, during the hottest time and highest light intensity of the afternoon it is better not to harvest, as the fruit may be under water deficit at that time. However, if the greenhouse environment is well regulated at optimum conditions, there will be less possibility of stress on the plants, even during the hot mid-afternoon. Later in the afternoon, when sunlight is less intense, is also a good time to harvest.

If you have a complete line of drying, sizing and packing equipment, the fruit will be dried during the packing process, so you could harvest earlier in the morning even if the fruit was slightly moist.

Most greenhouse tomatoes are harvested with their calyx remaining attached. This is a distinguishing characteristic of greenhouse vine-ripened tomatoes. The fruit may be harvested by hand, snapping the stem connection to the truss or using a pruning shears. It is important to trim the stem above the calyx to the level of the shoulder of the fruit to avoid having the stem puncture adjacent fruit when placing them in tote bins and during subsequent packing in boxes. If the greenhouse has hot water heating, plastic tote bins can be transported on carts running on the heating pipes. From the central aisle of the greenhouse they can be transported by tractor-pulled wagons to the packing facility. Use propane-operated tractors to prevent pollution in the greenhouse.

109. There are many ways of packing tomatoes. What packaging do you think is the best?

This depends upon your market. If you are shipping to a specialty market and receiving a premium price, your product should appear in a very high quality presentation. The fruit itself should be labeled. Be sure that the labels are attached in the same location on all the fruit. The best position is on the tip of the blossom end. If you have a very large operation and ship to wholesalers, you will need to have an automatic labeling machine. These machines do not place the label exactly on the blossom end.

Tomatoes are normally packed 20 pounds (9 kg) per box, in two layers. One very nice presentation involves the use of green paper containers, shaped like egg crates, with a cardboard separator between the two layers. Always size the fruit within each container. Do not mix small and large fruit; it does not give a good appearance. (Some growers are now shipping 15-pound boxes with a single layer of fruit.)

110. How can I overcome slow periods of the market, from mid-September to mid-October?

You can cluster-prune to three fruit per cluster to get heavier, larger fruit, bringing a premium price during the usually low-price period. While this could cause more fruit russetting, there should be less problem during the fall season when light and temperatures are less extreme. Also, before accepting a lower price, guarantee the product to your clients. If it should spoil due to slow sales you can replace the product free of charge. Some people have found specialty markets during slow periods, in processing salsas and dressings for which they receive a good price per pound.

111. What type of labels should I use on my tomatoes?

Use labels made of thin plastic with tear-off tabs. The consumer can easily remove them from the fruit without damaging the skin. Paper labels are hard to remove in one piece; they stick very tightly.

The labels should have a colorful logo representing your brand. Also many stores require a price lookup number (PLU). For greenhouse, large tomatoes, this number is 4799. Your boxes need to have the name and address of your company, brand name and logo, and country of origin.

112. When lowering my tomato plants, the stems often crack or break. How could this be avoided?

Several things will help to prevent the plant stems from breaking while the vines are being lowered (lowering helps to accommodate extra height as the plant grows). Try not to lower the plant more than two feet (0.6 m) at any one time. More frequent lowering and less distance at any one time will help, since with age, the stems become more brittle at the bottom. As mentioned in *Question No. 84,* it is best to support the bottom part of the stems above the growing bags or slabs with wire supports. These must be put in place prior to the first time the plants are lowered. The wire supports will help prevent stem breakage and will promote better air circulation around the base of the plants.

Lower the plants by unwinding some of the extra support string that you have previously wound on spools that slide along an overhead cable. Lower the plants all in one direction around each set of double rows to complete a "circle." The plants on the end will have to be curved around the end. Some growers place a 3-inch diameter drainpipe at the end of the rows to guide the stems of the end plants, as their stems are curved around to the other side.

Each time you lower the plants, you must move along the overhead support cable in the same circular direction. Bend all the rows in the same direction to prevent confusion when the plants are worked on. As mentioned earlier, under stringing plants (*Question No. 71*), always wind the supporting strings around the plant in a clockwise direction. Then, as the plant grows and the string is wound around the new growth, you will not mistakenly unwind the string already in place by not going in the same direction. This same principle applies to lowering of the plants— always move them around in a clockwise direction.

113. I have a greenhouse in Montana, and a very good market for tomatoes, especially during the winter months. What cropping schedule should I use for this area? Could a crop be grown over the winter months, using artificial lights?

Generally, in the more northerly latitudes, a single crop should be grown—seeding in late November, transplanting in late December or early January. Harvesting will start in March and continue until mid-November. Artificial lighting is really supplementary—not a substitute for natural sunshine. The capital cost of installing adequate high intensity discharge (HID) units is very high, and the cost of electricity and replacement of bulbs generally has not proven to be cost effective in the production of vegetable crops in greenhouses—even considering the extended day length. However, it is very important to install such lights in the seedling area and operate them for the five to six weeks of seedling growth prior to transplanting in the main greenhouse area.

114. It is the end of September, and I am planning to remove my tomato plants by mid-November. Is there anything I should do to prepare the plants for terminating the crop?

To keep photosynthates from moving into fruit that will not be harvested, it is best to remove the growing point of the plant 60 days prior to the expected date of pulling the plants. Some workers (D. F. Marlow, 1993, and J. C. Bakker, 1988) suggest that you remove all the suckers that may form on the plant thereafter except one. Leave one sucker immediately below where the plant is topped to help maintain the balance between generative and vegetative growth. When the sucker forms flowers, top it and allow another one to form, but at no time allow the flowers to develop. This will keep the plant generative and assist in fruit sizing up to the top of the plant. It will also assist in preventing fruit russetting (see *Question No. 133*). If fruit russetting becomes too much of a problem, do not top the plants. Keep all insects and diseases under control, as any population buildup will favor overwintering phases that could infest the new crop.

Pests, Diseases
and Physiological Disorders

115. My hydroponic system is a closed recirculation system, so I fear a disease may enter the nutrient solution and infect the plant roots. What can be done to kill these disease organisms?

One of the most severe problems of a closed system is the possible introduction of a disease organism that will enter the plant roots, reducing yields or even killing the plants. The most important of these organisms are the fungi: *Pythium*, *Fusarium* and *Phytophthora*. Prevention of water-borne organisms is feasible by means of several treatment techniques for sterilization of the raw water and nutrient solution. First, a system of ultraviolet, high-density water disinfection is available, such as that featuring "Priva Vialux" equipment. This system will control water moulds such as *Pythium* and *Fusarium*. It also controls bacteria and viruses. Another system of ozonation, followed by charcoal filtration is effective in killing many of these organisms. Finally, a sand filtration system reduces bacteria by between 95 percent and 99 percent.

The sequence of installation is: the sand filter, ozonation, carbon filtration and finally the ultraviolet, high-density water disinfection system.

When using ozonation, care must be taken to monitor the level of iron, as the iron chelate molecule is broken, causing its precipitation. It will have to be added on a continual basis after the nutrient solution passes through the ozonation system.

116. I have found fungal infection on portions of the plant stem where the leaves have been removed. It produces a gray-white fuzzy growth in these areas and later penetrates the stem, causing a brown rot to girdle the stem, eventually killing the plant. What is this fungus and how can it be prevented and/or controlled?

These are typical symptoms of gray mold (*Botrytis*). Once the stem of the plant is girdled by the infection there is little that can be done to save the plant. Cut the infected plant out and put it into a plastic garbage bag, being careful not to spread the spores into the rest of the crop. Some fungicides can be used to arrest the infection. If done soon enough, before it enters the stem, the plant can generally be saved.

Prevention of the disease is the best method of control. Fungal spores are moving in the air and when they land on a moist surface, such as a fresh cut or moist plant, they will germinate and penetrate the plant. The remedy then is to keep the greenhouse air within the optimum relative humidity of 70–80 percent. Remove the yellowing lower leaves up to the ripening fruit truss as soon as they lose color. Never cut the leaves with a pruning shears—always snap them off by hand at the abscission layer as pointed out in *Question No. 96*. This layer will dry and seal itself quickly, not allowing fungal spores to germinate should they contact it. When the leaves are cut off, within a half inch (1-cm) or so of the abscission layer, they will bleed creating an ideal environment for fungal infection.

Often I have seen cut leaves become infected with gray mold. Fortunately, most of the time the plant will shed this leaf stub at the abscission layer before the fungus can enter the stem. However, during cloudy, low-light conditions, the fungal growth will be favored and can grow quickly into the stem before the abscission layer forms a callus. Good ventilation and humidity control are the key factors in controlling the disease. Also, avoid breaking stems when lowering plants as this will open a port of entry to fungal spores. Cleanliness through the removal of leaves and dead, infected plants from the greenhouse is important to reduce the amount of fungal spores in the atmosphere.

117. I have noticed that some of the leaves of my tomato plants have small gray spots on the lower sides; they spread to pale areas and eventually brown spots. What is the problem and how may it be prevented and/or cured?

This sounds like leaf mold caused by the fungus *Cladosporium*. Similar to *Botrytis*, it requires moist conditions to infect the plant. Once again, avoid high humidity and practice cleanliness in the greenhouse. Some fungicide sprays are helpful. The disease is also spread by insect infestation, particularly sucking insects such as aphids and white flies. High populations of these insects cause a lot of secretion of plant juices to the surface of the leaves, creating moist surfaces favoring the germination and penetration of fungal spores. The insects also carry the fungal spores on their bodies, spreading the disease from one plant or leaf to another in their feeding frenzy. Control these insects through integrated pest management (IPM).

118. There are a lot of small white insects on my plants, particularly on the undersides of the younger leaves. What are they and how may I control them?

These insects are whiteflies. They are the most common pest of greenhouse tomatoes. They are easy to identify with their white powdery surface and triangular shaped body. They suck on the plants and secrete a sticky substance that favors leaf mold (see *Question No. 117*) and black sooty fungus growth. They suck on the leaves and fruit. When present on the fruit, they produce pin-sized yellow spots. High populations concentrate on the younger leaves of the plants, causing growth reduction and productivity losses. While they may be controlled by several pesticides, they quickly build up resistance. The most widely accepted method of control is through biological agents.

A small wasp, *Encarsia formosa*, lays eggs on the whitefly larvae and eat early larval stages of the insect. As the wasp grub eats the whitefly larvae, the larvae will turn black within two weeks, giving a good indication of success in its use. This predatory wasp may be purchased as pupae attached to paper strips from most greenhouse suppliers and companies selling beneficial insects. The paper strips containing 50-100 predators in blackened whitefly scales. Attach them to leaf petioles of the plants at the bottom of the canopy throughout the crop. A program of repeated introduction of the wasp must be initiated as soon as whiteflies are present.

119. I have a small population of whitefly present in my crop and want to purchase the wasp predators. I would like to know how many I should introduce into the crop to control the whitefly.

Release *Encarsia* at the first sign of whiteflies at the rate of two to three predators/square meter (10.76 sq. ft.) of greenhouse area. Some growers recommend, as a general rule, to use one predator/square foot/week (10/ square meter). Release them at weekly intervals until 80-90 percent of the whitefly pupae has turned black.

The time for this will vary depending upon environmental factors, prey population, etc. Keep temperatures and relative humidity at 73-81 F (23-27 C) and 70 percent, respectively, to favor the rapid growth and development of the predators (wasps). If the prey population is high, it may be necessary to introduce between one and five wasps/infected plant. Monitor weekly the number of whitefly and black scales. Obtain specific recommendations from the company providing the biological agents.

120. There are a lot of whiteflies in my greenhouse. Can I introduce the predatory wasps immediately or should I reduce the population of prey first by other means?

Do not use any residual pesticides for a month prior to introducing the predators. Reduce existing whitefly populations to less than one adult per upper leaf of the plant. Use nonpersistent insecticides such as M-Pede (insecticidal soap) or insect hormones. Charts such as the "Koppert Side Effect List" are very useful references to determine the danger and persistence of various pesticides on numerous beneficial organisms. Another very useful book on identification, life cycles, of pests and their natural enemies is *Knowing and Recognizing*. The chart and book are available from: G B Systems Inc., P.O. Box 39063, North Ridgeville, OH 44039-0063.

121. Are there any other biological agents to control whitefly without injuring predators?

There are a number of microinsecticides, produced by companies such as Mycotech Corporation. They use a number of bread molds (fungi) as insecticides: *Beauveria bassiana, B. brongniartii, Metarhizium anisopliae, Verticillium lecanii,* and *Hirsutella thompsoni. Beauveria bassiana* is marketed under the name "BotaniGard ES." It is effective on whiteflies, thrips, aphids, and other soft-bodied sucking insects.

Insects will not develop resistance to it and it produces no residue problems. It does not harm *Encarsia*; in fact, it has an additive effect in the control of whitefly by using both organisms. There is no harm to predators of the pests it controls.

If the spores are sprayed on the pests under relative humidity of 80-85 percent using three to four applications, five to seven days apart, effective control is achieved. You need a fine spray to achieve good coverage. The spray must contact the body of the insect (often on the undersides of leaves) for effective infection of the insect. The number of days for the fungi to kill the insect depends upon favorable environmental conditions that promote fungal spore growth and penetration of the insect's cuticle. Overhead sprinklers can wash the spores off. High temperatures, especially combined with low RH, will slow fungal growth or damage spores. It is best to apply this product in the evening, when RH will rise overnight. Fungicide residues, especially those containing sulfur, will kill the spores. Always follow the specific directions on the insecticide label—and its precautions when using with an IPM program.

The manufacturer's specifications indicate a 12-hour re-entry time and no pre-harvest interval. It should have no detrimental effect on bumblebees as long as it is applied at night and can dry on the leaves before bees enter. You could also lock up the bees in their hives at night before applying the fungus.

122. I have a difficult time watching out for insects in my crop. Is there some convenient, inexpensive method to monitor their presence?

To be successful with the use of integrated pest management (IPM), you must monitor pest populations, understand their various life cycle stages and know when to release the biological agents in order to best control pest populations at the various stages of their life cycles. Monitor the pest populations and keep records of the counts, the introduction of beneficials and their success in controlling pest populations. Monitoring the pest populations frequently is the basis for a successful control program. The predators must be introduced before the pest population becomes a problem. Daily observations and weekly counts indicate the dynamics of the predator-prey relationship, which indicates the success of the IPM program and guides you on what action must be taken to keep it in balance. If the pest population increases beyond control by the predators, it will be necessary to release large quantities of predators or to use an acceptable pesticide.

Sticky cards are used to monitor insect populations. These are 3-inch by 5-inch (7.5 by 12.5 cm) cards, coated with a sticky compound. These cards are available from greenhouse suppliers. Set the cards out when the seedlings are transplanted into the greenhouse. Place them at a minimum of one per 500-1000 square feet (46-93 square meters) of greenhouse area. The number of cards required will depend upon the crop, crop density and canopy, and pests present. With supported plants like tomatoes, cucumbers and peppers it is best to place the cards on the overhead strings, just above the crop. Because the plants grow and must be lowered, it is necessary to replace the cards weekly.

The reason for counting the cards every week is to obtain a representative sample of the population. The simplest procedure is to count all the cards once a week and then replace them with new ones. Place the counted cards somewhere else, perhaps lower in the canopy or along the central passageway of a large greenhouse, to act as traps. Be sure to place the new cards in different locations among the crop and not just sample counts from the same places in the greenhouse.

Inspect daily the undersides of leaves, the base and center of the plants, leaves near flowers and flowers themselves. Routinely inspect the plants as you walk along aisles or work with the plants. Instruct your helpers also to be vigilant as they carry out their daily tasks. Carry a small magnifying glass and notebook to make observations. Mark any outbreak of pests with a colored ribbon above the plants on the support string so that it is easily visible. Take positive action on these outbreaks immediately.

Make weekly assessments of your observations and relate these to what has happened with the insect populations monitored by the cards.

123. How may sticky tape traps be applied to reduce insect populations in the greenhouse?

Some of the larger greenhouses use 3- to 4-inch wide (7.5- to 10-cm) rolls of plastic tape commonly used as "caution barriers" at accident and construction sites. This tape can be set up with a bucket of sticky compound and rollers that will apply the compound to the tape as it is unrolled. The tape is strung along the posts of the greenhouse, wrapping it once around each post to support it at mature plant height. This is done before transplanting. It remains in the house for the entire period of the crop. If it becomes too thick with insects it could be replaced when the plants are lowered (if you are growing tomatoes). As long as the sticky tape is not near the flowers of the plants there should not be a problem with the bumblebees. If so, move it farther away or use another method.

124. I have notice that some of my tomato plants wilt badly during high light periods of the day. The roots are not a healthy white color, but have brown tips with some dieback. What is the cause of this and how might it be remedied?

This is probably a fungus root rot disease caused by *Fusarium, Phytophthora* and/or *Pythium*. Refer to *Questions No. 115* and *236* as to the use of silicone, hydrogen peroxide in the nutrient solution and the disinfection of recirculating nutrient solutions with ultraviolet light and ozonation.

Many tomatoes have resistance bred into the plants for some of these fungi. Check with the seed supplier as to what varieties are resistant. "Trust," "Match" and "Blitz" have resistance to *Fusarium* root rot.

A bioagent, "Mycostop," is effective in the prevention of *Fusarium* and *Pythium*. Mycostop is a fungus, *Streptomyces*, which produces natural enzymes and biochemicals that kill or repel plant pathogens. It is a wettable powder applied as a drench or spray to seedlings, or may be added to the nutrient solution at the rate of 2-5 mg/plant; refer to label for exact rates. In a drip irrigation system it can be applied at the rate of 1-2 gm/100 square feet of greenhouse. It has no problem with pH between 3 and 8, but you must avoid high EC. Under conditions where it is necessary to use high electrical conductivity of the nutrient solution, it will become necessary to reapply the bioagent after the EC has been lowered. When using hydrogen peroxide, add Mycostop separately when not delivering hydrogen peroxide. The manufacturer states that no safety pre-harvest period is needed as there is no risk of residues in the crop, and the reentry interval is only four hours. *Follow the manufacturer's directions in using this or similar products.*

Another product, "RootShield," which is a beneficial fungus *Trichoderma harzianum,* if applied as a drench to seedlings, will colonize growing plant roots and prevent root pathogens such as *Fusarium, Pythium, Rhizoctonia,* and *Sclerotinia* from infecting the plant roots. It is applied as a drench immediately after seeding at the rate of 8 oz/100 gal. (0.6 gm/liter). The product is claimed to provide long-term protection. *Again, follow the manufactuer's directions.*

125. Both green and black aphids are in my crop. What can I do to control them?

Aphids are relatively easy to control provided the populations are not large. If there are large numbers you will have to use an insecticide such as an insecticidal soap to reduce the population before introducing biological agents. Generally, aphids concentrate in the succulent upper leaves of plants, causing the leaves to curl under. This protects them, so when spraying you must use a fine spray with high pressure to get the pesticide onto their bodies under the leaves.

Adult aphids have both a winged and wingless form. They can easily move around within the crop, spreading new infestations. Workers in the greenhouse can carry them on their clothes from one area to another. Their life cycle varies from 7 to 10 days to three weeks, depending upon the environment. Under favorable greenhouse conditions, the shorter life cycle will result in rapid spread of populations. Aphids also secrete "honeydew" which favors leaf mold and sooty mold fungus diseases (see *Question No. 117*). The honeydew attracts ants, which protect the aphids by placing soil or other debris around the colonies. If you encounter a lot of ants on your plants look for aphids and control both with the use of pesticides. You may apply spot treatment if only localized infestation is present. As aphids are sucking insects they carry virus diseases into your crop. This can be very serious, especially in the case of European cucumbers.

Use parasitic fungi sprays such as "BotaniGuard" (*Beauveria bassiana*) or "Vertalec" (*Verticillium lecanii*) as general fumigations, and spot spray areas of high infestation with insecticidal soap (M-Pede), Enstar and Pyrenon, prior to introduction of the predators. Follow label recommendations.

Predators include lady beetles, lacewings and a midge larva, *Aphidoletes aphidimyza*. While ladybeetles and lacewings can assist in the control of aphids these predators are very migratory and tend to fly away when aphid populations are small. The midge larva should therefore be used as the primary controlling agent. Each larva kills 4-65 aphids during its 3- to 5-day development period. Biological agent supply houses recommend introducing the predator at the rate of 1 to 3 pupae per 10 square feet (1 sq meter) or 1 to 2 pupae per 10 aphids. Use the higher rates under higher aphid infestations. Repeat introductions three to four times, at weekly intervals. A parasite, *Aphidius colemani*, should be used in conjunction with *Aphidoletes aphidimyza* in the control of aphids. This tiny wasp lays eggs in aphids, mummifying them as they eat the aphids' body contents while maturing over a period of two weeks. You may observe the mummies to evaluate the effectiveness of the parasitic wasp. Release them at the first sighting of aphids at the rate of one parasite per 20-100 square feet (1-9 sq meters) of greenhouse area. Apply three to four times, at weekly intervals, and thereafter continue with one per 100 sq ft. *Follow closely the directions of the biological supply house.* Monitor the aphid populations weekly with yellow sticky cards as outlined in *Question No. 122.*

126. I introduced the predatory mite Phytoseiulus persimilis *into my crop to control the two-spotted spider mite. As they are both mites, how can I tell the difference between them?*

Mites are of the same class as spiders and ticks, so have four pair of legs rather than three as insects have. The two-spotted spider mite (pest) has two large black spots on its body. The male is oblong and slightly smaller than the female. The adult female is oval-shaped and rounded at the rear. Their color varies from light yellow to orange to reddish brown. Often the color of adults depends upon the crop they are infesting. They may be yellowish brown on cucumbers, but reddish brown on tomatoes. Spider mites move relatively slowly. With increasing temperatures, from 60 to 85 F (15-30 C), their development period is reduced from 33 to less than 7 days. Thus, high temperatures favor rapid population increases.

The adult predatory mite differs from the two-spotted spider mite in that it lacks the spots, is light red in color, has a pear-shaped larger body, longer front legs and moves quickly. In the temperature range of 70-81 F (21-27 C), adults develop from eggs within a week. This is twice as fast as their prey under these temperatures. Bright sunlight and higher temperatures are unfavorable for their development, so such conditions should be avoided, as these conditions favor the spider mite. A relative humidity of 60 percent or lower reduces egg hatching and increases development time of the predatory mite. A great deal of detail about and drawings of various pests may be found in *Hydroponic Food Production*, Fifth Edition (Resh: Woodbridge Press), available at most supply shops.

127. I have spider mites in my crop and wish to use integrated pest management to control them. What procedures should I follow?

If a large population exists (more than one mite/leaf) it is necessary to spray with short-term pesticides to reduce the population until only 10 percent of the leaves are infected. You can use "Vendex," "Torque" (fenbutatin oxide), "Pyrenone" or insecticidal soap as outlined on their labels to reduce the populations before releasing predators several weeks later. Introduce the predator *Phytoseiulus persimilis* upon the first observation of spider mites. Maintain optimum temperatures and relative humidity for the predators so that they may multiply faster than the prey (see *Question No. 126*).

Predatory mites come in shaker bottles so that they may be sprinkled evenly throughout the crop. They are also supplied in paper sachets, which can easily be attached to leaf petioles in the case of tomatoes. Release the predators in the early morning onto the mid- and upper foliage at the rate of one per square foot (8-10 / square meter) plus 10 predators per infected leaf, or as recommended by the biological supply company. Repeat introductions after two to three weeks. Once the predators have eaten all the prey, they will die. To prevent future infestations of the spider mite, it is possible to release some of the slower-acting, starvation-resistant predators *Metaseiulus occidentalis* in combination with *Phytoseiulus persimilis*. Maintain predator populations at one for every five prey. Monitor the spider mite populations once a week with the yellow sticky cards, as mentioned in *Question No. 122*.

128. I have found small white protuberances and "tunnels" between the leaf surfaces on some of the lower leaves of my tomatoes. Small white larvae are in these tunnels. What are they and how should they be controlled?

These symptoms indicate an infestation of leaf miners. The tomato leaf miner, *Liriomyza bryoniae*, is a common pest of tomatoes. More recently the American serpentine leaf miner (*Liriomyza trifolii*) and *Liriomyza huidobrensis* have become a problem with many greenhouse crops. Small yellow-black flies deposit eggs in the leaf, causing the pinpoint small white protuberances. As the eggs hatch into larvae, they eat these tunnels in erratic curves between the upper and lower leaf epidermis. The tunnels will coalesce as the population increases causing the leaves to senesce and dry. The mature larvae fall to the ground and in the folds of the plastic polyethylene floor barrier or folds of the growing bags where they pupate over 10 days to produce the adult flies. This cycle takes three to five weeks. High relative humidity (80-90 percent) favors egg deposition. The tunnels may be ports of entry for bacterial and fungal diseases. Also, the leaf miners can transmit viruses.

There are three parasitic wasps, *Dacnusa sibirica*, *Diglyphus isaea* and *Opius pallipes* that parasitize the leaf miner larvae. Both *D. sibirica* and *O. pallipes* lay eggs inside the leaf miner larvae, and the adults emerge from the pupae of the host. Both parasites develop more rapidly than leaf miners. The female *Diglyphus isaea* paralyzes the leaf miner larva and then lays one egg beside the host. The stung leaf miner can be recognized by the excrement it loses while becoming inactive. At temperatures above 59 F (15 C) the population of *D. isaea* grows faster than that of the leaf miners or the other two predators. It is therefore particularly useful at controlling its host at high tempera-tures. *Follow the suppliers directions*, but, in general, at the first sign of leaf miners, *D. sibirica* and/or *D. isaea* should be released at the rate of 0.5 parasites/square meter (one per 20 sq. ft.). The rate depends upon the level of infestation. Apply four times, at weekly intervals. The parasites are sup-plied together or mixed, as adults in shaker bottles. To moni-tor the level of parasitism and to identify the species, it is necessary to send leaf samples to a laboratory.

129. There is a lot of algae on the surface of my ebb-and-flow system for growing tomato seedlings. How can it be controlled?

Algae grows where it can get light and nutrients. The nutrient solution is an ideal source of food for it. Several steps will help to reduce algae. Light can be reduced at the surface of the beds by placing a black weed mat on top, under the seedlings. Allow the bed surface to dry be-tween irrigation cycles. Some growers recommend add-ing hydrogen peroxide to your nutrient solution at the rate of between 30 and 50 ppm. If the nutrient solution is being recirculated, as is the case with an ebb-and-flow system, treat the returning solution with ozone (see *Ques-tions No. 115 and 236*).

130. We have a greenhouse in a desert region, growing tomatoes. Frequently we encounter snakes in the greenhouse. How can we prevent them from entering?

Snakes enter the greenhouse to eat and sleep. The pres-ence of snakes suggests that there are mice in the greenhouse. Stop mice (and snakes) from entering by keeping all the perimeter walls well sealed to below ground level and keep doors closed tightly. Also, if you keep the greenhouse clean, free of plant debris and fruit, etc., there should be no food for mice and therefore they will not stay in the greenhouse and be an attraction to snakes.

131. I have heard that an extract from the neem tree is available as an insecticide. What is it and what pests does it control?

The product is Azatin or Neemix. It is effective in the control of fungus gnats, aphids, whiteflies, leaf miners and thrips. It is applied as a contact spray. Consult individual state regulations on pre-harvest time and crop approval.

132. Some of my tomatoes have sunscald, how can this be prevented? Is it advisable to apply shade during the high light summer months?

Sunscald is caused by direct sunlight touching the fruit while it is ripening. The light causes the skin to heat up and desiccate. Keeping the leaves on the plant around the ripening fruit can help to prevent this. Remove leaves only as they senesce, up to, but not above, the lowest ripening cluster. Shading the greenhouse during the warm spring months, starting in May-June and continuing until late September to early October, will help to prevent sunscald. Small greenhouses may use a 40 percent black or white plastic shade cloth placed on top of the polyethylene greenhouse cover. White shade cloth keeps the heat off the greenhouse. These shade nets have a UV inhibitor that prevents them from deterioration under high sunlight. Larger greenhouse operations often use whitewash paint on the roof. This washes off with the rain by the end of the early fall. If not, it will have to be removed with washing and use of a special cleaning agent. The better alternative for shading is to install an automatic shading system at gutter level, above the crop, within the greenhouse. This can be operated by a computer system monitoring the sunlight intensity from a weather station on top of the greenhouse roof. Generally, the shade cloth will be pulled across the supporting cables only during the midday period during maximum light levels.

133. During poor sunlight periods I find that some of the tomatoes have small cracks, and a brown coloration on the skin in the area of cracks. What is the cause of this poor fruit quality?

This physiological disorder is termed russetting. There are a number of potential causes for the disorder, including having too few fruit on the plant, rapid changes in environmental conditions and irregular or non-optimum irrigation cycles.

Keep between 26 and 32 fruit on the plant at all times. If you thin the clusters to only three fruit each, there will be problems of russetting. If the plants are very vigorous, more russetting will occur as the fruit expands very rapidly. The cause is believed to be the rapid expansion of the internal tissue with slower expansion of the skin, causing too much stretching, resulting in rupture of the skin.

Keep temperatures constant in their optimum day-night ranges. At night, 62-68 F (16.5-20 C) and day, 70-72 F (21-22 C). Keep environmental conditions constant, relative humidity, light patterns, temperatures and irrigation cycles all affect this condition. Plants should not be allowed to dry so much as to cause wilting between cycles, because when water is applied it will rush into the plant, due to its large water deficit. This water will be directed quickly into the fruit, causing the fruit contents to expand more rapidly than the skin, which can stretch, causing cracking.

134. I have noticed that some of my tomatoes form deep cracks on the shoulder of the fruit and, at the same time, the shoulder of the fruit is green or yellow with a leathery appearance. What is the cause of this malformation?

This discoloration is sunscald, caused by direct sunlight hitting the fruit as it ripens. This will occur under very high light or if you prune lower leaves above the ripening trusses. It may be necessary to shade your greenhouse, using whitewash on the roof or an internal automatic moveable shade screen above the plants. This would be controlled by a computer in conjunction with its monitoring of light conditions from the weather station on the top of the greenhouse. Prune lower leaves only up to the ripening fruit as mentioned in *Questions No. 79, 95* and *96*.

The large fruit cracks on the tomato shoulder are due to irregular irrigation cycles as discussed above in response to *Question No. 133*. Do not allow the plants to suffer excessive water deficit, as when the next irrigation cycle occurs, a rapid uptake of water into the fruit causes rapid fruit expansion causing cracking. Irrigation cycles must be more frequent during the midday period, under high light conditions.

Some varieties are more susceptible than others to fruit cracking and the "green shoulder" ripening disorder. However, your choice of variety is also dependent upon other factors such as fruit size, disease resistance, plant vigor, etc.

There does not exist an ideal plant with all the desirable genetic characteristics. Hopefully, this ideal will be achieved in the future with research tools such as genetic engineering.

135. Some of my tomatoes have a leathery black, sunken skin on the blossom end of the fruit. My watering cycles are sometimes irregular; could that cause it?

During early stages of this disorder the affected fruit will have a green, water-soaked appearance which sinks into the fruit. As the symptom progresses, it produces a brown leathery tissue at the blossom end. This is termed blossom-end-rot (BER). Irregular watering is one cause of the disorder, by inhibiting calcium uptake. Other causes include root diseases that kill the plant roots and thereby reduce water uptake or produce a calcium deficiency. Poor aeration and lack of oxygen in the plant roots cause root dieback, which also will result in BER.

This problem can become very serious, causing a lot of fruit spoilage. The remedy is to neither over water nor under water. Do not let the plants wilt between irrigation cycles. Check the roots for fungal infection and treat them promptly. Also, monitor the calcium levels in the nutrient solution and plant tissue, with nutrient and tissue analyses. If a calcium deficiency exists, increase the calcium level of the solution and possibly use a foliar application of calcium nitrate.

136. Some growers tell me not to remove fruit having blossom-end-rot. Is that procedure correct?

While in the past this bad fruit was removed immediately, growers now suggest that it could be counter productive to do so, for several reasons. First, it might cause a rapid flow of nutrients to the remaining fruit, causing fruit cracking and/or russetting (see *Question No. 133*). Second, with less fruit load, the plant may become vegetative.

137. I have noticed that some of my tomatoes have protuberances while others are large and oblong in shape with large scars at the blossom end. What causes these fruit deformations?

This distortion of fruit is called roughness and catfacing. Symptoms include wrinkling of the fruit shoulders and walls, protuberances and indentations. Poor pollination due to low temperatures and high relative humidity causes abnormal fruit development. It is a very common problem on the lower trusses of the plants, and especially with greenhouses having unit heaters as a heat source. Unless that heat is ducted to the bottom of the plants, the lower part of the plants will experience cool temperatures and high relative humidity, with poor ventilation.

The solution is to maintain temperatures and relative humidity at optimum levels. Hot water heating with the heating pipes at the base of the plants is the best source of heat. Unit heaters require polyethylene ducting at the base of the plants to bring the heat down and allow it to rise up through the crop canopy. This will also improve ventilation and reduce the relative humidity. Once the plants are large enough to necessitate the removal of the lower leaves, the ventilation will be increased at the base of the plants and this problem will be reduced.

138. I have some insects in my crop, which is going to be removed shortly. Should I spray before removing the plants or simply dispose of the insects with the plants?

It is very important to kill all pests before removing your plants. Using approved procedures, fumigate with approved pesticides having a short residue of four to six weeks, because when you place the next crop in the house you will want to reintroduce biological control agents. The objective is to eliminate the insects so that they will not overwinter in cracks and hidden spaces within the green-house, awaiting the next crop.

Several days before removing the plants from the greenhouse, pull them out so that they will dry somewhat, reducing the weight of the material to be moved. Pull the roots out and stop the irrigation system, but leave the plants hanging from their support strings to dry. You can save the plant clips for reuse one time, if they are not brittle. Pry them apart with a knife or spoon and then soak them in 10 percent bleach solution for several hours to disinfect them. Dry and store them for use with the next crop.

Be sure to dispose of the plants far from the green-house. It is best to place them in a pit and then bury them to prevent any eggs hatching and fungal spores from dis-seminating back to the greenhouse on the next crop.

139. How should I clean my greenhouse between crops?

It is very important to remove all plant debris from the floor. In general, it is best to replace, between crops, even the black-on-white 6-mil floor barrier used in most greenhouses. This will eliminate a lot of fungal spores, insect eggs and pupae. Prior to removing the polyethyl-ene, spray it with a formalin or bleach solution. Also, spray all of the walls and bases of the greenhouse where insects may be overwintering. Allow at least two weeks to dry and air before bringing in new plants.

Methyl bromide is the most effective agent against in-sects, weeds, nematodes and fungi. However, it is very toxic to humans and must be applied only by trained per-sons, using approved safety gear and observing all official regulations and procedures. Aeration for 10 to 14 days after application is required before planting.

Lettuce and Herbs

Water Culture Systems

140. What varieties of bibb lettuce would you recommend for hydroponic culture?

The choice of variety will depend on your climatic conditions and, sometimes, your market. In warmer climates such as Florida, it is important to have a variety resistant to *Pythium* root disease. Some of the more common varieties include: Deci-Minor, Ostinata, Cortina, Cometa, Milou, Titania, Rachel and Cortina. There are, however, many more varieties than these offered by numerous seed houses.

141. I want to grow lettuce in a semitropical to tropical climate. I understand that there are a number of different water culture systems available, but do not know which system would be best for my conditions. Any suggestions?

A number of water culture systems would be suitable to your climate. Both the gutter NFT or pipe system and the raft, raceway or floating system can be used. The choice will depend upon several factors. The availability of water is especially important with the raft system as large volumes are needed to keep the beds full of nutrient solution. If the quantity of water is limited by well capacity or other source restrictions, such as pipe diameter, it may be better to use the gutter NFT system, which requires a lower volume of water. Of course, the main advantage of the raft system is that, by using a large volume of water, the temperature of the water may be regulated more evenly than with the gutter NFT. Maintain the nutrient solution temperature between 70 and 75 F (21-23 C) with the installation of a water chiller in the nutrient tank. The water chiller cools, aerates and circulates the solution.

The styrofoam boards, or "rafts," which float on top of the water in the beds, reduce the amount of heat entering the solution. At the same time, they support the plants.

However, the raft system also has a number of disadvantages, the most important of which is the cost of the beds. These beds need to be extruded from a specific mold, which may not be available. There will then be the additional cost of a custom mold and the difficulty of finding a company capable of making it. Shipping of the beds would also be expensive, as they are large. They come in lengths of approximately 10 feet and must be glued together. The glue-joints often crack, causing leakage of nutrient solution.

The system must sit on level ground or, preferably, a concrete floor. This is costly and, with limited access to the plants, it is difficult to monitor and treat your plants for outbreaks of diseases and insects. For these reasons, I would recommend using the gutter or pipe NFT system.

Again, much information about various systems, with numerous illustrations may be found in *Hydroponic Food Production* (Resh: Woodbridge Press).

The greatest challenge with the gutter NFT system is to keep the nutrient solution at optimum growing temperatures. There are several ways to assist in maintaining lower solu-

An NFT gutter system with movable tape with holes for insertion of plants. Tape is drawn by power away from the operator as he inserts the transplants, and toward the operator as he harvests. The author is examining lettuce plant roots for any possible *Pythium* infection with Frank Armstrong, owner of F. W. Armstrong Ranch, Oakview, California.

tion temperatures. First, as mentioned for the raft system, you may install a chiller in the nutrient tank. Second, make the gutters short in length, about 12 feet (3.6 m). Give them a good slope of two percent to keep the solution flowing from the inlet to the catchment end. The gutters should be mounted on galvanized steel tubing benches four feet (1.2 m) high. If the gutters are only 12 feet long you can lift them out with all of their plants to obtain access or to harvest. Locate the nutrient tank underground. This will help to keep the solution cooler.

High temperatures, in excess of 75 F (23 C), favor *Pythium* fungal infection of the roots. As mentioned in *Questions No. 115, 147* and *236,* the use of potassium silicate, ozonation of the returning solution and hydrogen peroxide may all assist in its prevention.

142. I recently found a gutter NFT system for sale at a bargain price. What crops could be grown in such a system?

The gutter system was originally designed for the growing of European bibb lettuce. Red oak leaf, romaine and other leaf lettuces may be grown successfully in this system. Basil does well in the system. Be sure to start the seedlings for these plants in growing cubes of rockwool, or Oasis cubes, and transplant to the channels after about two weeks once the plants form several sets of true leaves. Spinach, especially baby spinach; that is, spinach harvested relatively immature, can be produced with this system. Be careful, however, that it does not get overwatered.

143. To increase production of bibb lettuce in my greenhouse can I grow a series of beds one above the other?

Some growers have tried this, but unsuccessfully, due to lack of light reaching the lower tiers. However, it is possible if you use a system of NFT channels supported by an A-frame structure that will permit light to reach the lower tiers. A problem is the high cost of constructing such a system. It would work in high solar areas or during the summer months of more northerly latitudes, but there will be insufficient light during winter months in northern areas. Under poor light, the lettuce will not form heads and will become very leggy.

144. I wish to grow European bibb lettuce in a gutter NFT system. What is the limitation on the spacing and what distance between plants and rows should be used?

Spacing of your plants is limited by available light for their growth. If plants are spaced too closely, mutual shading of neighboring plants can result in insufficient light entering the crop, and many of the lower leaves will yellow. This will reduce the productivity of all the plants.

When plants are young (up to two weeks after transplanting) it is possible to keep the gutters touching each other; then, later, spacing them apart as the leaves of adjacent plants contact each other. This "accordion" fashion, moving your gutters apart with increasing plant growth, will permit you to fit more plants into the greenhouse.

The final spacing must be eight inches (20 cm) between rows. The spacing within the rows remains constant, with plant holes located at 7.5-inch centers. Based upon total greenhouse floor area, with allowance for a central aisle, plant density will be two plants/square foot (21 plants/sq m).

145. I have a lot of two-inch diameter PVC pipe available and would like to make a pipe NFT system for growing lettuce. At what spacing should I drill the holes in the pipe, and of what diameter?

Make the hole centers at eight inches (20 cm). Be sure to keep them oriented at the same level on the pipe, in a straight line. A drill press would help a lot in making the holes. Make the diameter of the holes large enough to allow the growing cubes to enter the pipe. The diameter will be equal to the diagonal length of the square rockwool or Oasis cubes.

146. Growing lettuce in a gutter NFT system, how may I keep the growing channels cool, besides chilling the nutrient solution in the cistern?

One method is to direct the cold air from a cooling pad and fan system under the tables supporting the NFT channels. This can be done by placing deflector panels on the inside of the cooling pads and mounting fan jets in a closed chamber under the deflection panels. Perforated polyethylene tubes attached to the fan jets, running under the benches, will blow cold air under the benches. If the perimeter of the benches is closed, with a polyethylene drop curtain, the cold air will be forced upwards past the plants.

147. On my seedling tables for lettuce, sown in rockwool cubes or Oasis cubes, there is a lot of algae growth from the nutrient solution passing during irrigation cycles of the ebb-and-flow system. How could this be prevented?

Placing a black fine screen or weed mat on top of the table under the seedlings will help in reducing the algae growth by reducing the light on the surface of the tables. Also, if the mat can dry between cycles without the seedlings suffering lack of water, the growth of algae will be reduced. That is, schedule the irrigation cycles only as often as required by the seedlings and only during daylight hours.

Recently, the use of hydrogen peroxide has been introduced to control algae. Use 5 ppm in NFT of lettuce. Use the 35 percent form presently used in the dairy industry. It is put directly into the nutrient solution tank, or it can be injected from a separate stock tank.

148. Growing lettuce in an NFT channel system, I have noticed that the plants at the inlet end look larger and greener than those at the outlet end of the channels. What is the problem?

This often occurs due to nutrient and oxygen gradients along the channel. The inlet end will have the highest levels of oxygen and nutrients, depleting as the nutri-

Spacing of bibb lettuce at 8-inch (20-cm) centers. Note that the sequence of planting is such that each set of three beds is transplanted about 12-13 days apart to permit better light penetration into the crop. The lettuce matures in 35-40 days after transplanting. Courtesy of F. W. Armstrong Ranch, Oakview, California.

ent solution travels along the channel to the outlet. This may be corrected in a number of ways. First, reduce the length of the channels so they do not exceed 50 feet (15 m). The shorter the channels, the fewer problems will arise and the easier it will be to handle them when harvesting. If individual channels are to be moved during harvesting, they should not exceed 15 feet (4.6 m). Second, install an oxygen pump, with air stones (like those in fish tanks), added to the tank to increase the oxygen level of the solution. Finally, the slope of the channels should be two percent.

149. When transplanting my lettuce into a three-inch diameter PVC pipe NFT system, many of the seedlings wilt from lack of water, even though there are adequate watering cycles. What could be wrong?

The problem here is that, if the plants are not set down sufficiently, the water does not touch their base. To avoid this problem, commercial NFT gutters have ribs on the bottom surface of the channel. This keeps the nutrient solution flowing directly under the plants rather than meandering around them. In a pipe system, the nutrient solution level may not be high enough, especially on the inlet end, to reach the base of the plant-growing cubes. This can be resolved by placing a small strip of paper towel or capillary mat across the channel under each plant.

150. I live in Southern California, which has lots of sunlight year-round. How many crops of hydroponic bibb lettuce should I be able to grow annually?

Hydroponic bibb lettuce takes between 30 and 35 days to mature after transplanting, depending on the variety. From the time of sowing to transplanting the seedlings will require about two weeks. If the seedlings are started in a separate seedling house, the main greenhouse will be used only for the maturing crop, so this two-week seedling stage will not be part of the greenhouse cycle. Daily seeding and harvesting must be carried out to keep a continuous cropping cycle. In general, for the climate of Southern California you should achieve 10 crops per year. Of course, these crops will be rotated over an area in relation to the number of harvests and plantings you need per week to meet your market demand.

151. I wish to grow strawberries in the greenhouse. I understand that they could be grown in a pyramid pipe NFT system. Is this the best system for growing strawberries?

The pyramid or A-frame NFT system was designed to increase the number of lettuce plants that could be grown in a given area of greenhouse by making use of the vertical space. The A-frame allowed plants to receive sufficient light by reducing shading of one tier from the one just above it. This water culture is suitable for lettuce but creates root oxygenation problems for strawberries, as they have a long cropping cycle of five to six months—in contrast to the one-month cycle of lettuce. Also, fruiting crops tend to suffer more from oxygen deficits than do low-profile leafy crops such as lettuce.

For strawberries, I recommend a vertical system, using a substrate such as peatlite mixes, coco core, perlite mixes, and rice hull mixes. The vertical culture may be plastic sacks, stacked pots or a modified vertical pipe system. In the pipe system, plant the strawberries in 4-inch diameter plastic pots and place them in the pipes for support and drainage. At the end of the production season in May-June you can sell the strawberry plants as bedding plants to outdoor backyard gardeners.

Baby Salad Greens

152. I want to grow hydroponic baby salad greens for mesclun mixes. What plants should be grown?

Generally, mesclun mixes are composed of some of the following plants (the specific components depending on the type of flavor desired for the salad mix): Arugula, Beets

(Bull's Blood), Broadleaf Cress, Chervil, Chicory, Dill, Fennel, Mizuna, Red Giant Mustard, Red Leaf Amaranthus, Red Orach, Red Russian Kale, Spinach (varieties – Hydra, Joker, Kerdion), Tah Tsai, Upland Cress and numerous varieties of lettuce are used in these mixes. It is important to use both red and green lettuce varieties. Reds include Dark Red Lolla Rossa, Red Oakleaf, Cimarron (Red Romaine), Redina, while greens include, Green Romaine (Paris Island Cos) and Tango.

153. When growing these baby salad mixes, what percentages of each should be grown?

The percentage of each component depends upon the mesclun mixes to be prepared by yourself or the wholesaler to which you market. A general guideline is to grow about half lettuce and the remainder a mixture of the others with a larger proportion of beets and spinach.

154. Which hydroponic methods are most suitable to baby salad mixes?

The choice here depends upon cleanliness. As these crops are sown close together and the tops cut at an early stage, it is important that during harvesting the product does not retain any substrate on it. I have tried rice hulls which grew the crops well, but created problems during harvesting by adhering to the leaves. A peatlite medium would present similar problems. It is not economically feasible to use rockwool or any growing cubes due to high cost. Perlite, like peat and rice hulls will adhere to the plants during harvesting.

NFT, using gutters, requires sowing seeds in rockwool or Oasis cubes, which are too expensive and will not give you sufficient plant density. The cleanest method I found was to use pea gravel.

155. How should I set up my hydroponic system to grow baby salad mixes?

It is very important to have a clean floor. You may pour a concrete slab for the floor, but that is costly. An alternative is to add 4" to 6" (10-15 cm) of sand fill to the soil floor and then cover it with a black weed mat which will prevent weeds from growing, yet allow water percolation.

Install benches for an ebb-and-flow hydroponic system. Movable benches would be best as you will be able to utilize almost all of the floor area of the greenhouse. Fill the benches with two inches (5-cm) of pea gravel. Do not use smaller than quarter-inch diameter igneous gravel, as smaller particles will adhere to the crop leaves when harvesting. This is a closed or recirculating system. A cistern tank, pumping system, plumbing and controller will be some of the components of the irrigation system. Refer to *Question No. 115* regarding sterilization of the returning nutrient solution.

156. What is the best method of sowing the seed for baby salad mixes? Should I raise seedlings and later transplant?

These plants will be ready within three weeks of seeding, so they will only reach two to three inches (5-7.5cm) in height by harvest. They are sown very close together, so it is not possible to sow in cubes and, later, transplant. It also would be too costly. Sow the seed directly into the gravel medium.

157. At what spacing must I sow my baby salad crops?

A general rule for plant spacing of these crops is: red items, sow in rows three inches (7.5 cm) apart with about an eighth-inch (0.3 cm) between seeds within rows. For green crops, the spacing between rows is three inches and within the row the seed may be touching. Within the rows the seed should fall in a band about one inch (2.5-cm) wide, not just a single row of seed. This can be done by hand, using a wooden lathe as a guide. The wider spacing for the red plants is to permit more light to enter the canopy; required for obtaining a red color.

158. I am growing baby salad crops, using an ebb-and-flow system. Is my regular lettuce formulation suitable for these crops?

The lettuce formulation should be okay for the baby salad crops. I have used the following formulation with success on these crops in Southern California:

> N – 150 ppm
> P – 40 ppm
> K – 180 ppm
> Ca – 230 ppm
> Mg – 50 ppm
> Fe – 5 ppm
> Mn – 0.5 ppm
> Zn – 0.1 ppm
> Cu – 0.035 ppm
> B – 0.5 ppm
> Mo – 0.05 ppm

It will be necessary to reduce the nitrogen levels under cloudy conditions or the plants will become too succulent.

159. What is the growing period of baby lettuce and beets, and how often may they be harvested before reseeding?

These baby salad crops in general have a three-week cropping period from time of sowing seed to harvesting. The beets may be harvested at least twice before replanting. Most lettuces can be harvested only once.

Sow crops in sections to obtain continuous harvesting, at least three times per week. These cropping cycles will depend upon your market demand.

Harvest the plants when they reach two to three inches (5-7.5 cm) in height. The consumer wants a very tender product. Cut them with a sharp knife or scissors, placing them directly into boxes, which must be refrigerated immediately. They are very delicate and perishable.

After the final harvest, remove the plants from the beds immediately, pulling up their root systems. If the plants get too old they will form a large root mat at the bottom of the gravel, making it difficult to remove. Beds can be sterilized with a 10 percent bleach solution between crops. Just be certain that the sterilizing and rinsing water does not get back to the nutrient tank.

160. I am sowing my lettuce and other baby salad crops directly in gravel beds. How can I maintain proper moisture so that the seeds will germinate?

To achieve good germination the seeds must remain wet, but not waterlogged. You could place a sheet of polyethylene over the top of the beds after seeding and watering, but this reduces oxygen, raises temperatures and is time-consuming. The best method is to install an overhead misting system operated by a controller. Mist has to be applied during daylight hours every 30 minutes for 30 seconds. The seed must not dry out at any time. The mist lines above each bed must be on individual solenoid valves to enable their independent operation, only for the germination process and initial plant development, for a period of 7 to 10 days.

161. How often does my baby salad crop in the ebb-and-flow system need to be irrigated?

The frequency of irrigation cycles will be a function of the stage of plant growth, the temperatures, relative humidity and sunlight conditions. As the plants form more leaf area they will require more water. Under high light, high temperatures they will require more water due to high evapotranspiration rates. Irrigation cycles should be automated with a moisture sensor or at least a controller. I have successfully used cycles in Southern California during the summer months—every two hours with ten minutes for each cycle. During the morning and early evening, when light is less intense, periods may be increased to three hours.

When the mist system is operating for seed germination, usually for 7 to 10 days until the first true leaves emerge, less frequent irrigation cycles will be required.

162. I do not receive much weight of product from my crop of baby salad greens. What is the average expected production?

These salad greens, harvested at very early stages, do not weigh a lot. The average field production for three-week cropping is one-third pound (150 gm) per row-foot, where a row-foot is three square feet (0.3 sq. m) of bed area, containing three rows of plants. From my experience I found that hydroponic greenhouse production for a three-week crop averaged 0.15 lb/sq. ft. (730 gm/sq. m) of bed area, in comparison with field production of 0.11 lb/sq. ft. (540 gm/sq. m). This is about 35 percent more production.

Herbs

163. I am interested in growing herbs hydroponically. What are some of the more popular culinary herbs?

While most culinary herbs can be grown hydroponically, it is not economically feasible to grow some of them, due to their long cropping period and/or competing large field production, which generally depresses prices. Some of the more common culinary herbs are: anise, basil, chervil, chives, coriander (cilantro), dill, fennel, fenugreek, marjoram (oregano), mints, parsley, rosemary, sage, savory, tarragon and thyme. While most of these may be used fresh or dried, the higher market value is for fresh herbs. Hydroponic herbs will be very clean and of high quality for the fresh market. They should be properly packaged to prevent spoilage. Of the mints, spearmint (*Menta spicata*) has most demand. Parsley, dill and cilantro are produced in large field operations in the southwestern U.S. and now in Mexico, so the price is often depressed. As rosemary is a woody shrub, which grows for many years, I would not recommend it for hydroponic greenhouse culture. Fenugreek is also field-grown.

Anise, various basils, chervil, chives (including Chinese chives), baby dill, fennel, oregano, spearmint, sage, savory, tarragon and thyme may be produced hydroponically. Besides Italian large leaf or sweet basil, others such as Thai basil, cinnamon basil, lemon basil and purple basil have specialty markets. Presently, a lot of Italian basil coming in from Mexico is depressing the price.

164. I wish to grow basil, mint, oregano, thyme, tarragon and chives hydroponically. What type of soilless system would you recommend, and can they all be grown in the same culture?

I do not recommend the same culture for all of them, as some are very sensitive to moisture and require a well-drained substrate. Basil can be grown in NFT canals, perlite, peatlite or rice hull mixes. For the NFT system you must sow seeds in rockwool or Oasis cubes, as for lettuce. In the other substrates, basil can be directly sown in the medium. Basil does not like a lot of moisture at its stem base (crown), so it must be kept above any moisture, or in a relatively dry medium. Mint, on the other hand, is tolerable to moisture as long as it receives adequate oxygen in its roots. Mint produces underground stolons, which spread through the substrate, therefore, would be somewhat constricted in NFT channels. It does well in substrates like peatlite, perlite and rice hulls. It also grows vigorously in a modified NFT capillary mat system on benches. However, it is important to control algae in such systems as pointed out in *Questions No. 129* and *177*. The other herbs—oregano, thyme and tarragon—like a well-drained substrate. Chives will grow in all of these substrates, including NFT and sand.

For efficient space utilization in the greenhouse, it is best to have benches, or floor beds, with at least four inches (10 cm) depth of medium. A drip irrigation system using T-tape spaced at four to six inches (10-15 cm) apart, operated automatically with a time-clock controller, is basic to the system. Normally, when using one of these substrates, including sand, the solution is not recirculated. Stock tanks with an injector system are the most practical method of irrigating.

Use hydrogen peroxide in the nutrient solution to assist in the control of algae (see *Question No. 129*).

165. I have heard that watercress will grow very well hydroponically. What is the best method of growing it, and is it a profitable crop to grow in the greenhouse?

Watercress is very well adapted to water culture, as that is how it grows naturally. The best method is a modified NFT system using a capillary mat. The capillary mat is needed to spread the water laterally in beds. Ground or raised beds may be set up in the greenhouse after covering the greenhouse floor with a weed mat. This modified NFT is a recirculating system. A nutrient cistern tank, pump, piping and controller are some of the components of the system.

The small watercress seed may be sown directly on the capillary mat using a "whirlybird" hand seeder. Install an overhead misting system to germinate the seed. Be careful not to overwater, as flowing water will wash the seed into pools or out of the beds. An alternative is to have a seedling bed. This can be the same as the other growing beds, but instead of using capillary matting, place about 1 inch of pea gravel in the beds. Sow the seed directly into the pea gravel with the whirlybird seeder. Apply mist during germination, with overhead mist nozzles. As the seed is very small, you must be careful not to let it dry between misting cycles. Use more frequent cycles of 10 minutes or less, depending upon environmental conditions. Duration of cycles should be about 15 seconds.

Transplant the seedlings when they are about three inches (7-8 cm) tall (about three or four weeks after seeding). Simply pull them with their roots attached from the pea gravel, place in plastic tote bins and transplant directly on top of the capillary matting of the growing beds. Moisten the capillary matting well before transplanting. Set plants at one-inch centers on the mat. You do not have to be exact, as they will all grow together in time. Mist the transplants for at least a week until they root. Circulate the nutrient solution through the beds at the same time.

Mint grows well in a modified NFT system using a capillary mat. A thick root mat forms at the base. Courtesy of California Watercress, Inc., Fillmore, California.

Mint ready to harvest. Courtesy of California Watercress, Inc., Fillmore, California.

Chives growing in a sand and rice hull mix. A drip
T-tape irrigation system is used. Courtesy of
California Watercress, Inc., Fillmore, California.

Thyme growing in a rice hull substrate. Courtesy of California
Watercress, Inc., Fillmore, California.

It takes about three to four weeks to first harvest; there-after harvest every 28 to 30 days, depending upon light conditions. During the hot summer months the watercress will go to seed after one to two cuttings, so you will have to replace the plants more often. Set up a continuous program of seeding and harvesting daily.

Yields should reach between 0.4 to 0.6 lb./sq. ft. (2-3 kg/sq. m). Even at these yields it may be questionable as to the economic feasibility of growing watercress in green-houses in competition with field production. If a stable market demand and price can be obtained from a niche marketplace, combined with high quality and very attractive packaging, it can be done.

166. I am going to grow hydroponic watercress in my greenhouse and would like to know what nutrient formulation would be suitable.

You could start with this basic formulation which I have used successfully in the production of hydroponic watercress. You will have to adjust the formulation according to your specific environmental conditions. With experience, you will be able to develop a fairly optimum formulation. Watercress does need a lot of iron, so I generally use 5 ppm of iron in the nutrient solution. It is best to add perhaps 2-3 ppm of iron twice per week, instead of adding 5 ppm only once.

N – 160 ppm	B – 0.3 ppm
P – 45 ppm	Mo – 0.03 ppm
K – 200 ppm	
Ca – 175 ppm	
Mg – 50 ppm	
Fe – 5 ppm	
Mn – 0.8 ppm	
Cu – 0.07 ppm	
Zn – 0.1 ppm	

Watercress seedling beds with pea gravel substrate. Solenoid valves in front of the author are for injecting nutrient solution and raw water into beds. Courtesy of California Watercress, Inc., Fillmore, California.

Watercress seedlings 5-6 days after sowing in pea gravel propagation beds. Courtesy of California Watercress, Inc., Fillmore, California.

You must keep the watercress vigorous, but not too succulent, or it will be damaged in post-harvest handling. Refer to *Questions No. 36, 45, 92* and *100* regarding the adjustment of nutrient formulations and environmental conditions.

167. At what temperatures and relative humidity should watercress be refrigerated?

Watercress must be refrigerated at 33-35 F (0.6-1.7 C) with a relative humidity of 95-100 percent. It must be dry before packaging. The best method of cooling and drying is with vacuum cooling. The temperature of the watercress must be lowered immediately after harvesting as it spoils very quickly as temperature rises. When harvesting, place the product in plastic boxes that have slits or are meshed so that good air circulation within the container will facilitate cooling. Place the boxes immediately in refrigeration.

168. I am growing hydroponic mint. How often do I need to replace the crop?

You should be able to keep the mint growing for one year. After that, the root mat becomes so thick that the plants suffer for good oxygenation and productivity falls. Harvest every four to five weeks. Do not allow the mint to grow above six inches (15 cm) in height, as it will lodge, causing rot of stems and leaves below. This will result in death of plants and reduced productivity.

169. What is the best method of starting mint plants?

Mint takes several months from seeding until it is ready to transplant. With your first crop, you probably have no source of plants, so you will have to start from seed. Sow seed in 125- to 200-celled flats with a peatlite propagation mix. Sow five to six seeds per cell. Once seedlings reach about 1½ inches (3-4 cm) in height they will be ready to transplant. When transplanting, retain the root balls to reduce the transplant shock.

Mint may be propagated from shoot cuttings. If you have an existing crop and wish to change it, take cuttings for three to four weeks prior to removing the crop. Use shoots that are clean and free from diseases and insects. Cut shoots about four to five inches (10-12.5 cm) long in the greenhouse, placing them in boxes, keeping them moist. Make the final cuttings in a separate propagation area of the greenhouse. Recut the shoots to three to four inches (7.5-10 cm) long, making the cut directly below a leaf node. Leave about four to five leaves on the cutting. Stick the base of the cuttings in a Number 1 rooting hormone powder and then immediately place them into 100- to 200-celled flats containing a peatlite propagation mix.

The flats need to be placed in a special propagation house, having an automatic misting system and below-ground heating on raised benches. The benches should contain about four inches (10 cm) of sand on top of the heating cables or hot water pipes to evenly distribute the heat and allow good drainage. The cuttings will take about four weeks to root. When transplanting, space the mint plants at 3-inch by 3-inch centers.

The first harvest will take place after four to five weeks. It will take three to four harvest periods before the plants have multiplied to optimum plant density and maximum productivity.

170. How should I plant basil in my peatlite hydroponic beds?

Basil may be sown directly into the peatlite medium at four-inch by four-inch (10 by 10-cm) spacing. After two harvests the branching plants will require wider spacing to eight-inch by eight-inch (20 × 20 cm) by removing every other plant. Alternatively, sow the seedlings in 100-celled flats with a peatlite medium. Transplant when they reach 1" to 1½" high to the growing beds at six-inch by six-inch (15 × 15-cm) spacing.

After three to four harvests, the basil becomes woody and forms a lot of flowers. The crop should be replaced at that stage. Always remove flowers early by pinching with your fingers. This will help to keep the plants more vegetative, forming many shoots.

Pest, Diseases and Physiological Disorders

171. My watercress, growing in a NFT capillary mat system, develops a lot of small floating weeds. What are they and how may I prevent them?

These floating weeds are duckweed. They are a severe problem due to their consumption of a lot of nutrients, and they retain surface moisture, attracting algae and fungus gnats. You must prevent their introduction by sterilizing plastic tote bins, knives, etc. with a 10 percent bleach solution. Once the weeds are introduced, it is very difficult to control without closing down your system and cleaning all of the beds. The weed is circulated with the nutrient solution in a closed system. Filters on the returning solution to the tank will assist in preventing its spread. Between crops, treat the beds with a herbicide and sterilize the capillary mat with a 10 percent bleach solution. Wash and dry the matting or replace it.

172. The leaves of my herbs are being chewed during the night. I find a lot of waste (detritus) on the leaves where they have been eaten, but I cannot find any insects. What might this be?

This damage is a result of cutworms (larvae of moths) feeding on the plants during the night. In the day they drop down into the medium and hide. Caterpillars (larvae of butterflies) feed on plants day and night, so can be easily found during the day. If you look under the plants and in the substrate you will find them.

Otherwise, visit the crop at night to find the insects. These can be controlled with pesticides such as Lannate, Pyrenone, Malathion, etc. (depending upon what is approved for your crop). Refer to pesticide labels for rates and crops approved. Biological control may be achieved with Dipel (*Bacillus thuringiensis*), a parasitic bacterium. It must be sprayed weekly on the plant surface. The cutworm and caterpillar larvae must ingest the bacterium for control. The larvae will die after about five days. Repeated application is essential for control. The bacterium is said by the sellers to be harmless to mammals and leaves no toxic residue, which could affect predators.

173. I have found some whiteflies, aphids and larvae eating my baby salad mixes. How can I control them?

With salad crops like these it is not possible to use biological agents, as they would be present on the harvested product. So, use more conventional pesticides, but use as many natural ones such as Dipel, Vertobac, insecticidal soap (M-Pede), BotaniGuard, etc. as possible. Others, such as Pirimor and Pyrenone, are acceptable as long as they are approved for the crops and have a very short residue and pre-harvest period. *To repeat, with all insecti-*

cides, pesticides, fumigants, etc., note the labels and follow
the manufacturer's directions and local regulations.

174. I have found some powdery red-orange spots on the stems and leaves of my mint. What is this and how can it be treated?

This is rust, a common fungus disease of mint. It must
be controlled quickly or it will spread through your crop.
Use a sulfur-containing fungicide such as Thiolux. Note
labels and be careful with Thiolux, as it is persistent, with
a 30-day pre-harvest period. Thiolux is also effective
against powdery mildew, another common disease of mint.

175. My herbs have whiteflies and aphids. What can I use to control them?

With herbs like the baby salad greens, it is difficult to
use biological predators, since, as mentioned above, they
will be present on the product when harvesting. It is better to use nonpersistent insecticides such as Pyrenone,
Pirimor and insecticidal soap (M-Pede). Dipel, Vertobac,
BotaniGuard, Mycostop and other microorganism sprays
may be used, provided they are approved for the crops in
question. Most of these pesticides have a one- to two-day
pre-harvest period. *Note labels, follow instructions.*

176. My lettuce has large pieces of upper leaves missing, as if torn off. It occurs at night. What is happening?

I expect you have mice in the greenhouse. Set mouse-
traps near the crop and look for holes in the greenhouse
where they may be entering. Keep the house clean. Look
for mice droppings to identify the problem. Mice carry
disease, including Salmonella bacteria, which could con-
taminate your crop.

177. Is algae in my herb beds a problem?

Yes. Algae is a problem in your herbs for several reasons. Algae consumes nutrients from the nutrient solution. It also causes accumulation of moisture, creating very favorable conditions for the growth of insects such as fungus gnats, and for snails. The larvae of the fungus gnats feed on the plant roots and the snails eat the leaves.

178. When I walk past my herb beds which grow in a capillary mat NFT system, I find many small black flies in the air. What insects are these and how should they be controlled?

These are adult fungus gnats. If you wave your arm above the beds they will fly up and you can feel them to get an idea of the population. Yellow sticky cards are used to monitor the insect population (see *Question No. 122*). They may be controlled with some pesticides such as Pyrenone. Other natural insecticides include Azatin or Neemix (see *Question No. 131*), extracts from the neem tree. Another effective control is Vertobac, a *Bacillus* bacterium similar to Dipel. Note labels, follow instructions for approved crops and rates of application.

There are also parasitizing nematodes, *Steinernema feltiae, S. bibionis* and *S. carpocapsae*, that control fungus gnats by entering the larvae. The nematodes are applied in water as a drench, spray, or in the irrigation system. They may be applied as a preventative or when fly larvae are present at the rate of 50 million nematodes per 100 square meters (1076 sq. ft.).

179. My bibb lettuce does not form heads properly; they are too open. What causes this?

There are several reasons for loose heads. The temperatures may be very high, in excess of 80-85 F (27-29 C). Lower the temperature, possibly by installing evaporative cooling pads, with exhaust fans or a fogging system. Check the potassium levels. If potassium exceeds 200 ppm, this will prevent head formation. If light levels are poor, heads will not form. Do not overlook the need for carbon dioxide enrichment, especially under poor light conditions. Generally, these levels should be between 1000 and 1200 ppm.

180. The tips of my lettuce are brown. What causes this, and what can be done to stop it?

This is a common problem with some varieties of lettuce—termed "tip burn." Physiologically, it may be a lack of calcium in the leaf tips or rupture of cells caused by high temperatures and low relative humidity. Keep the greenhouse environment at optimal levels of RH and temperature. Maintain RH between 65 and 80 percent. Day temperatures should be from 65 to 70 F (18-21 C) and night temperatures between 55 to 60 F (13-15.5 C). Heating the nutrient solution to a minimum of 60 F (15.5 C) will reduce tip burn. But do not heat the solution too much, as, once it approaches 70 to 75 F (21-24 C), the high temperature will favor the growth and spread of *Pythium* fungus. Some varieties are resistant to tip burn.

European Cucumbers

Cultural Practices

181. I wish to grow cucumbers in Florida. What varieties would you recommend, and why?

Cucumbers in Florida suffer from powdery mildew. It is important to use a resistant variety such as Marillo, Discover, Millagon, TW242, Tyria and Kalunga. The first four varieties are from De Ruiter Seeds and the last two from Enza Zaden (both are Dutch seed companies). These varieties are termed mildew tolerant. However, they are susceptible to leaf necrosis under poor light conditions. With the high light levels of Florida it should not be a problem.

182. Since cucumber seeds are very expensive, how should they be seeded to obtain good germination?

It is best to sow cucumber seeds in one-inch rockwool cubes or Oasis cubes. Place one seed per cube in the small quarter-inch holes. Cover the holes with coarse vermiculite, to retain moisture and assist the germinating seed, in removing its seed coat.

183. When should cucumber seedlings be transplanted?

After the cotyledons fully open and the first set of true leaves are visible (about three to five days), transplant the cubes to the larger rockwool blocks measuring 3 × 3 × 2.5 inch (7.5 × 7.5 × 10 cm). Use the blocks with the large holes, in which the cubes will fit. Depending upon the light conditions of your area, transplant to the slabs within two weeks, once the plants have two fully unfolded true leaves, with the next set emerging.

184. I have found a few of my cucumber seedlings smaller and thinner than the rest. Should I transplant these?

No, you must start out with very healthy plants. Smaller ones will not catch up to the others. Set the smaller plants aside to grow a little more. If they improve their growth rate and stature to that of healthy plants within several days you can transplant them last. Otherwise, in case you become short of transplants, keep them for possible replacements for the odd plant that may be damaged in transplanting. Still, if these weaker plants do not pick up in vigor very quickly they will not be usable.

185. My cucumber seedlings form a thick mat of roots at the base of the rockwool blocks. Is this a problem for the seedlings? If so, how could they be grown better?

The cucumbers should be discouraged from forming a thick root mat at the base of the blocks as many will be damaged during the process of transplanting. The roots need to be air-pruned (see *Question No. 58*) by placing the blocks on wire mesh benches, such as movable benches, or with the use of slats such as "snow fencing." Water overhead with a hand-watering wand or with sprinklers, using a half-strength nutrient solution. Also, keep the blocks spaced at four inches by four inches (10 × 10 cm) by positioning the blocks corner-to-corner in a checkerboard pattern. If the plants are grown beyond the fully formed first true leaves, they will become entangled unless spaced wider apart. In areas of low winter light levels, it is recommended to keep the seedlings in the propagation area, under artificial lighting, until they reach 12 to 16 inches (30-40 cm). At that time they will form a thick root mat under the blocks. The plants will need to be staked.

In areas of good sunlight, transplant much earlier, when the first set of true leaves fully expand (about two weeks from seeding).

186. What precautions should I take when transplanting my cucumbers?

Cleanliness is of utmost importance in the transplantation process. It is very easy to break roots in transporting them from the seedling area to the growing houses. Any such damage is an easy entry for fungal diseases, such as *Fusarium* and *Pythium*. Disinfect all trays, wagons, etc. with a 10 percent bleach solution prior to moving the plants (see *Question No. 69*). Water the seedlings well before moving them and immediately place the irrigation emitter on the block once the transplant is placed on top of the slab or growing bag.

187. How large should I make the holes in my slabs on which to set the transplants?

They should be the same size or slightly smaller than the blocks to prevent algae from growing in exposed areas. As mentioned in *Question No. 208* use the special tool that is available to cut the holes. The diameter of the holes that the tool makes is somewhat less than the diagonal of the blocks.

188. Due to the susceptibility of cucumbers to crown rots where should the emitters be placed?

To prevent crown rots and gummy stem blight, keep the base of the plants dry. Place one emitter on each block by staking it at the corner and through to the slab below to secure the block in position. Do not allow the emitter to drip onto the base of the plant. Within 7 to 10 days the plants will root into the slab or bag below. At that time the emitter should be moved to the slab, close to the block.

189. How should I string the cucumbers when transplanting?

Have all of the strings attached to overhead cables before transplanting. One convenient method I found to secure the string at the base of the plant is to pass the end of the string under the growing block when setting it on the slab or growing bag. Wrap the string around the plant in a clockwise direction and attach a plant clip to the stem of the plant immediately under a true leaf.

190. I find that the stems of some of my cucumbers are so thick that they are restricted by the plant clips. What can I do to prevent this constriction?

This constriction of the plant stem can reduce movement of nutrients and water uptake and result in productivity loss. At the same time, any damage to the stems will be a port of entry for fungal diseases. Eliminate this problem by using larger, one-inch plant clips made especially for cucumbers.

191. What is the standard method of supporting cucumbers?

They should be supported differently than tomatoes. Tie strings to the overhead cables, but do not leave any extra length, as the cucumbers need not be lowered. Wrap the string around the stem (about one wrap between each leaf) in a clockwise direction, and use vine clips every few feet to help support the plant. Cucumbers grow very quickly so it is necessary to string the plants at least twice a week. If the growth gets ahead of you it will be very time-consuming to later string them, as they become tangled together with their tendrils.

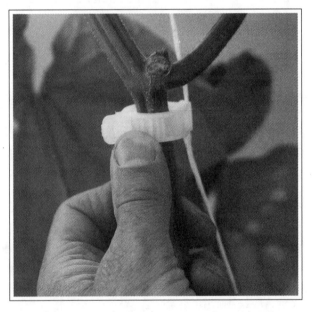

Use of plant clips to support cucumber vines. Place clamps directly under a leaf with hinge pinching the support string.

192. I am unsure as to which rockwool slabs are best for European cucumbers. What would you recommend?

Use wider slabs for cucumbers than for tomatoes. The eight-inch (20-cm) wide slabs are recommended for cucumbers, as the cucumbers are more vigorous than tomatoes. Use the 36" × 8" × 3" (90 × 20 × 7.5 cm) slabs. It is also better to use the high-density slabs, as they will maintain their structure better than the normal ones.

193. How should the rockwool or perlite slabs be spaced for cucumbers?

Cucumbers are planted at a density of 1.2 to 1.4 plants per square meter (10.76 square feet) of greenhouse area per plant. For larger operations, this is a population of 5000 plants per acre, or 12,500 per hectare. Plant two plants per slab 24 inches (60 cm) apart. Place slabs six inches (15 cm) apart, end-to-end. This gives a constant spacing of 24 inches within rows. Space slabs in double rows, separated 2-2.5 feet (60-75 cm), with the drip lines feeding both rows from a three-quarter-inch diameter black polyethylene lateral running between the rows. Aisles are six feet (1.8 m) wide, with 2.5 feet (75 cm) center-to-center of double rows of slabs. This gives two rows per 8.5 feet width (2.6 m) of the greenhouse. Slabs may be arranged in single or double rows, but keep the plant density the same. With single rows, use the V-cordon training system. (See *Question No. 197.*)

194. I have found water accumulating at the base of some slabs. Is this a problem for the plants?

Yes. This accumulation of water will cause root aeration problems as well as be a source for algae, fungus gnats and diseases that these insects may carry onto the plants. The slabs need to be level across, and along their length. A very slight slope toward the drainage ditch between double rows is acceptable, provided it does not exceed one-fourth inch (0.5 cm). Water will not collect on the inside of the slab, as that is where the drainage slits are made to conduct the leachate away from the slab. If sloped in the opposite direction, water will accumulate at the base of the plants, creating oxygen deficit. Level the floor and walkways as indicated in *Question No. 239.*

195. When training my cucumbers, what do I remove?

Cucumbers are trained to a single stem, going up to the overhead wires. Remove all the suckers and tendrils in the leaf axis. Tendrils wind around leaves and fruit, crinkling the leaves and deforming the fruit. Remove them by hand with a quick snap similar to the small suckers. Suckers should be removed when they reach about 1½ inches (4 cm). Remove the tendrils also while they are very small, about four inches (10 cm) long.

196. What is the method of fruit removal on the principal stem?

It is important to have a good balance of fruit on the main stem. Too many fruit will reduce the vigor of the plant early in its life cycle, and it will not be able to regain this vigor. Many of the small stem fruit have to be removed to leave only four to five fruit on the first 20 nodes (6.5-7 ft.) of stem height (usually nodes 10, 13, 17 and 20). Often, two fruit will develop in the leaf axis. Always remove the smaller one. Fruit to be removed must be removed very early, when it is about one inch long. Remove the fruit by hand.

Remove the small stem-fruit on the main stem of cucumber plants up to 4 to 5 feet. Then allow fruit to form on nodes 10, 13, 17 and 20 of the main stem before training the plants over the support wire.

197. How should the cucumbers be trained as they reach the overhead wires?

European cucumbers are trained under two systems: the V-cordon system and the renewal umbrella system. In the V-cordon system, two support wires are placed 6½ to 8 feet (2-2.5 m), or at gutter height, above the floor. The wires are spaced 20 inches to 28 inches (50-70 cm) apart. Plants are inclined alternately into the aisles with support strings tied alternately to the two overhead wires. With the renewal umbrella system, the main stem is cut one leaf above the overhead wire allowing two laterals to form at top. These two laterals are permitted to grow two-thirds of the way down the main stem. Allow all the fruit to develop on the laterals as they grow down. When all the fruit develop, a next set of laterals will form near the support wires. Once the fruit has been harvested from the first laterals, cut them back to the overhead wires, just below the others that are developing. This procedure is repeated with each set of subsequently developing laterals.

You must remove all suckers, tendrils and any second sets of fruit developing in the leaf axis. Each lateral should produce five to seven fruit. Further information on the training of various crops, including cucumbers, is available in *Hydroponic Food Production* (Resh: Woodbridge Press).

198. When twisting the main stem over the overhead wire, it sometimes breaks. How can this be prevented?

Cucumbers are very delicate. Their stems break very easily. Handle the plants very carefully, not forcing the plant tips around the support strings too tightly. There are special plastic stem supports available, which hang from the support wires and hold the top of the main plant stem.

199. I have a cucumber crop in Florida, where they grow very rapidly. Which system of training would you suggest I use here under these high light conditions?

In Florida, or other southern regions having high light conditions year-round, it will be necessary to train the cucumbers differently. A modified renewal umbrella system or V-cordon system should be used. The training of the main stem is the same, but as the plants reach the overhead wire, allow only one sucker to grow instead of two (see *Question No. 197*).

200. Some of my friends growing cucumbers tell me that I should remove some of the leaves above the overhead wire. Is this correct, and if so why?

Removing a few of the leaves above the overhead wires will permit more light to penetrate the plants. It will improve ventilation, reduce fungal diseases and improve the growth of the fruit on the laterals. Cut the leaf petioles with a pruning shears. Do this only if your plants have a dense canopy of leaves above the wires, and if you have good sunlight, but do not expose fruit to the sunlight.

201. Some of the lower leaves of my cucumbers are yellowing. Should they be removed, and how?

These yellowing leaves must be cut off with a pruning shears to improve ventilation at the base of the plants. In regions such as Florida, having high light, temperatures and relative humidity with abundant vegetation everywhere, there is a severe problem with diseases and insects. Sucking insects such as aphids, white flies and thrips carry viruses from outside crops and plants into the greenhouse. Some viruses carried from melons spread into the cucumber crop, causing a lot of damage and reduced productivity. The insects must be excluded as much as possible from the greenhouse with insect screens, and those entering must be eliminated through the use of pesticides and biological agents.

Some cucumber growers in Florida have used a milk dip for cleaning their pruning shears between plants. Workers carry a small container of milk on their belts and dip the shears after working on each plant. The lactic acid is believed to be effective in arresting the spread of viruses. There are also some plant varieties which have tolerance or resistance to these viruses.

202. When the fruit are maturing, is it important not to remove blossoms from the fruit tip?

Yes. Generally, removing blossoms from the maturing fruit can cause the fruit to be malformed with a thick end rather than a nice, rounded, somewhat pointed tip.

203. Is there a problem with pollination of cucumber flowers by bees?

Pollination of European cucumbers should be prevented. It will cause the fruit to swell in sections of the fruit, giving it a nonmarketable quality. Most recent varieties are "all female" having no male flowers so that pollen is not present. However, sometimes a male flower may form, especially on varieties that are not "all female." Also, any seed formation in the fruit makes the fruit bitter in flavor.

204. What is the best stage of harvesting cucumbers. How do I know that they are ready?

The fruit should have visible ridges. Normally, measure the diameter of the fruit with your second finger and thumb forming a loop to pass over the fruit. This is okay with experience, but, to be more accurate, use a gauge having various diameter holes to indicate the correct diameter for harvesting. The color must be a dark green. Do not allow the fruit to begin yellowing, as they will be overly mature. Depending upon the variety, they may be between 12 and 16 inches (30-40 cm) long. They must be straight to be of high quality.

205. How should the fruit be harvested?

It is best to harvest the fruit in the mid-morning when the fruit and plant foliage are dry. Cut them off with a pruning shears within one-eight inch (3 millimeters) of the shoulder. As mentioned in *Question No. 201* use a milk dip for your shears between plants, if there is any presence of viruses in the plants. The fruit should be harvested into plastic tote bins and transported to the packing shed, in larger operations with a tractor and wagon, for immediate packing. Be careful not to bruise them in transport.

206. In my rockwool culture of cucumbers the leachate from the slabs is about 10 percent. Is that sufficient?

With rockwool culture the duration of irrigation cycles should be long enough to obtain between 20 and 30 percent leachate (runoff) from the slabs. This level of leaching is necessary to move nutrients through the slabs so that the salts will not accumulate. At the same time, the solution will bring oxygen into the slabs as it flows past the roots. Most rockwool culture is an open system. The slabs must be slit at the inside edge at several locations between the plants, not directly under them. This will provide adequate drainage, which must be conducted away from the base of the slabs through slits in the black-on-white 6-mil polyethylene floor barrier. The excess solution percolates through the soil or the sand fill underneath, to a drainage system that takes it away from the greenhouses to a holding pond.

207. How often should I measure the leachate, and what is a good way of doing it?

Check the runoff from the slabs several times a day and keep records of the percentage leachate. To simplify this task, construct a special collection tray. Place it under a slab having two normal plants representative of the crop in their vigor and growth habits. The collection tray needs to drain into a bottle for measuring the volume of leachate. At the same time, place another bottle under an emitter to monitor the volume per emitter entering the slab. Multiply the emitter volume times the number of emitters on the slab (two-one at each plant), and then divide the volume of the leachate by this emitter volume to calculate the percentage leachate.

208. I find it is a very tedious job to cut the holes in the slabs to place the rockwool blocks. Is there an easy method of doing this?

Yes. Cutting cross slits by hand is slow, and damaging to the slabs. There is a special tool available. You press down and it swings a razor around, cutting a circular hole in the polyethylene liner. This tool should be available from the rockwool supplier.

209. A greenhouse supplier told me that I need a "start tray" to automatically operate the irrigation cycles. How does this tray function?

The start tray is an important piece of equipment in controlling your irrigation cycles. This tray will respond to environmental changes through the uptake of nutrient solution by the plants. This is a stainless steel tray that is placed under a slab that has two healthy plants within the crop. The bottom of the wrapper of the slab is cut off and the slab, with the rest of the liner, is set on top of a piece of capillary matting in the tray. The tray has a V-shaped groove in the bottom where the leachate accumulates and makes contact with an electronic sensor. The sensor electrode sends a signal back to the computer or controller to stop an irrigation cycle. It works on the principle that as long as the sensor contacts the solution in the tray the electrical circuit is complete and it prevents the irrigation cycle from occurring. As the solution level in the groove falls, with its uptake by the plants, the circuit is broken and an irrigation cycle will be initiated. Adjustment of the probe level will determine the moisture level within the slab. As the probe is raised it will increase the irrigation cycles. The duration of the irrigation cycle is preset on the controller so that, when the cycle is initiated, it will last for that length of time.

210. How often should I check the EC and pH of the leachate and slabs? What is the best method of sampling the slabs?

Check and record the EC and pH at least twice a day. Record the position of the slabs selected. Generally, test the pH and EC of two to three slabs at random through- out the greenhouse. Take an extract of the slab solution, using a plastic syringe, available from suppliers of rockwool. Take samples from under the block in the zone of most active roots. Do not test the leachate, as this is a mixture of solution from under and between plants where there is less uptake activity. You should have a pH and EC monitor installed downstream, but close to the injector. Record these values at the solution monitors several times a day.

211. I have found high levels of conductivity and non-optimal pH values of my slab solutions. What should I do to correct these levels?

First, test a number of slabs throughout the crop to substantiate these findings. It could be that some emitters are partially plugged, causing the slab to dry and thus insufficient leaching will result in accumulation of salts. If that is not the problem and most of the slabs have the same high levels, you must leach the slabs to bring the pH and EC within acceptable levels. Avoid lowering the EC too quickly (may cause fruit cracking in tomatoes). Do not leach with "raw" water as it often contains some elements such as calcium, magnesium, iron and perhaps sodium chloride. These elements will be added to the slabs as you leach and thus put the ratios of the various elements out of balance. At the same time, any sodium chloride will accumulate, as the plants will not take it up. Other nutrients such as potassium, nitrates and phosphates will be depleted during leaching with raw water, causing an imbalance within the slabs. The more you leach, the closer the slab solution will approach that of the feeding solution.

212. Is my tomato nutrient formulation suitable for cucumbers?

No. You must use a special cucumber formulation. Refer to books such as *Hydroponic Food Production,* by the author, and also seek advice from the suppliers of rockwool. Cucumbers generally use a two-level formulation, with one level at about half the concentration of the mature formulation. The lower level formulation is used until the first cucumbers have set. Some workers (D. H. Marlow, 1993) suggest using three formulations rather than two. A phase I formulation from week 0 to 7, phase II from week 7-11 and phase III after week 11, when fruit on the laterals begin to develop.

The basic changes are in the levels of nitrate, potassium and calcium. The level of nitrate and potassium are reduced about 15 percent in the third phase. Calcium is lowered seven percent in the third phase. These changes are based upon lowering the EC of the solution as light conditions improve during spring in the more northerly latitudes. Adjustments of these formulations will have to be made to balance generative and vegetative phases of the plants under variations of environmental conditions, especially light levels as discussed in *Questions No. 91, 92* and *100.*

213. During cloudy weather should I adjust the EC of the nutrient solution?

Yes. During cloudy weather you want to make the plants work (apply a little stress). Do this by raising the EC of the nutrient solution, but do not raise it as high as for tomatoes. It is recommended to raise the EC of the slab to between 2.5 and 4.0 mMho.

214. In the more northerly areas what type of cropping schedule should be followed?

Cucumbers in these areas are grown as either a single crop or two crops annually. For a single crop, sow seeds in a seedling house with artificial supplementary lighting December 1. Transplant to slabs or bags in the greenhouse during late December. By the first week of February start harvesting fruit. Continue harvesting until mid-November. During the last half of November remove plants, clean up, etc.

For a two-crop system, seed the first crop December 1st and transplant in late December, with first harvest by early February, as with the single cropping schedule. However, remove the plants by mid-June. Sow the second crop in June in a separate seedling house or range and transplant within three weeks, continuing the crop until mid-November.

215. What annual production of cucumbers should be achieved?

The annual production depends upon how well you manage the plants and their environment and the available sunlight in your region. The industry average is 110 cucumbers per square meter (10.76 sq. ft.) to 140 or higher for better growers. This is equivalent to 10 to 13 fruit per square foot, or 73 to 93 per plant.

Another basis for evaluating production is that one

should obtain between 2 to 2.5 fruit per week per plant during the harvesting stage.

216. I have just removed the plants from the greenhouse. My greenhouse is heated with hot water boilers so I can use steam sterilization of the rockwool slabs. What procedures should I follow?

The rockwool slabs may be used for several crops, provided they are sterilized correctly, without damaging their structure. For this reason, it is better to purchase the high-density slabs, as they will maintain structural integrity better than the regular ones. Some growers will use the same slabs up to three years. There will always be some losses due to handling, etc., but that should not exceed 10 percent annually. After removing the plants from the slabs and the plastic wrappers, lay the slabs on their edge to facilitate drying—that will make it easier to handle them. Move them onto pallets in the center passageway (concrete floor) of the greenhouse. Stack the slabs flat to about three feet (1 m) in height, being sure that successive rows are perpendicular to the each other. Allow about four inches (10 cm) between each slab so that the steam may circulate through the pile. Cover the palletized slabs with a steam tarp and place a thermometer in the center of the stack to monitor the temperature. Maintain the temperature between 175 and 212 F (80-100 C) for at least 45 minutes.

After the slabs have cooled and completely drained they may be re-sleeved. Be sure to replace the white-on-black polyethylene floor liner before setting out the slabs. If you are growing more than one crop per year, it is possible to keep the existing polyethylene floor liner without replacing it, provided that it is sterilized with a 10 percent bleach solution or three to five percent formaldehyde solution between crops (formaldehyde gives off a toxic gas, so use approved protective precautions and equipment). Any torn areas in the floor liner will need to be replaced.

It is possible to sterilize the slabs with sunlight. Prepare them in the same way as for steam sterilization then place them outside in the sun under polyethylene covers for the summer months. Using this method, you need a second set of slabs to start the fall crop. This assumes that you are using a two-crop annual schedule.

217. I am presently changing my crop. How should I clean up the greenhouse and its components?

Prior to removing the plants, after all harvesting is completed, apply Dibrome by spraying or painting it onto the heating pipes. Maintain greenhouse temperatures about 77 to 80 F (25-26 C) for 12 hours. *Always be sure to check with your state regulations as to the use of any pesticides, and also follow manufacturer's directions.*

Other products to clean the greenhouse include 10 percent bleach solution, three to five percent formaldehyde solution (this gives off toxic gas, so use proper precuations and protective equipment). D. H. Marlow (1993) suggests using quaternary ammonium chloride salts (Q-salts). These include products such as Greenshield, Physan 20, Consan 20, Prevent and Triathlon.

It is also important to clean the irrigation system, especially the emitters, which become plugged by deposits during their use. A two-percent solution of concentrated nitric acid (that is, 60-70 percent, in its original concentration) will remove chemical deposits. Keep the lines full for 24 hours, then flush with raw water. Be extremely careful with nitric acid; use the protective procedures and equipment recommended by the supplier. To eliminate biological agents, D. H. Marlow (1993) recommends using an 11 percent commercial sodium hypochlorite diluted to

1:350. Let them stand for 24 hours and flush afterwards, as was done with the nitric acid solution.

Environmental Conditions

218. What is the optimum relative humidity for my cucumber crop? Is there a difference between day and night?

The optimum relative humidity for cucumbers is 85 percent, slightly higher than for tomatoes. Some workers have found that fruit color of cucumbers is reduced under high relative humidity conditions lasting 24 hours per day. They suggest that the nighttime humidity should be lower than that of the day. If guttation of the plant leaves occur during the early morning, it indicates that relative humidity is too high, with the air becoming saturated. With strong root pressure, the plant takes up water faster than it can use it in transpiration. As a result, special cells at the margins of the leaves excrete drops of water.

Growers now use the term vapor pressure deficit (VPD) to measure the ability of the air to dry objects in the environment. Vapor pressure deficit is the difference between the actual concentration of water vapor in the air and the maximum possible at a given temperature. As the temperature of the air increases it can hold more water. The greater the VPD, the greater will be the evapotranspiration rate of the plants. That is, the rate of water movement from the plant leaves to the surrounding air in the greenhouse will increase.

If the plants are unable to take up sufficient water to meet the loss through evapotranspiration, they will wilt. As suggested in *Questions No. 89-92* and *100*, there is an optimum VPD for plants bearing fruit to keep them under slight stress, in order to maintain the plants in a generative state of growth.

219. What are the various optimum temperature regimes for the growing of cucumbers during their growth stages?

During germination the temperature of the growing media should be from 81 to 82 F (27-28 C). Germination will occur within two days. D. H. Marlow (1993) proposed the following temperature regimes for cucumbers. Upon germination, the air temperature should be 75 to 77 F (24-25 C). After transplanting to the blocks, the air temperature should be lowered to 73 to 75 F (23-24 C). Maintain a temperature differential between day and night of 3 to 5 F (1-3 C). Further lower the temperature by several degrees as the plants continue growing in the blocks. Before moving the plants to the greenhouse growing area, reduce the temperature in the propagation area to 68 F (20 C) and 72 F (22 C), night and day temperatures respectively. This should be done for several days prior to transplanting to harden the seedlings. Once the plants are placed on the slabs, keep the temperatures at 70-75 F (21-24 C) day and 62-68 F (16-20 C) night. Use the lower temperatures of these ranges once the plants reach the overhead wires.

220. To cover the floor, can I use clear or black polyethylene?

No. Black polyethylene would cause a buildup of heat and clear polyethylene will transmit light, favoring weed growth underneath. Use white-on-black 6 mil polyethylene to reflect light up into the crop. This light reflection is particularly important in areas having limited sunlight, especially during winter months.

221. My greenhouse is heated with unit heaters. I notice that the base of the slabs is cold. What could be done to improve root temperatures?

It is very important to maintain the temperature of slabs for cucumbers relatively constant from 65 to 68 F (18-20 C). Place ½"-¾" (1-2 cm) thick styrofoam under the slabs to insulate them from the cold floor. It will also help to duct the heat from the unit heaters down through the center of each row of plants, using 12-inch (30-cm) diameter polyethylene convection tubes. A hot water bottom-heating system, using a loop of small tubing under the slabs, will help to maintain optimum root temperatures.

222. I find that in the early morning the margins of the plant leaves are wet. What is this?

This is guttation (see *Question No. 218*), caused by high relative humidity combined with high root water uptake. Reduce the relative humidity, especially during the night and early morning.

223. Is carbon dioxide enrichment beneficial for cucumbers?

A concentration between 800 and 1200 ppm carbon dioxide in the greenhouse atmosphere is considered optimal. While ventilation is important in controlling relative humidity and temperatures, it does not substitute for carbon dioxide enrichment. Good ventilation will permit carbon dioxide to enter the leaves through the stomates more efficiently by breaking the stagnant air layer immediately surrounding the leaf surface. However, even on bright, sunny days with lots of ventilation, the plants are not satisfied in their need for carbon dioxide under such rapid growing conditions. During cloudy winter months, the crop may deplete the carbon dioxide level within several hours, thereby reducing plant growth.

224. I remove a lot of flowers during the thinning of my cucumber plants. Is there anything that could be done with these?

I have met some growers who have developed a so-phisticated market for the flowers along with the miniature fruit. The flowers have a lot of nectar, making them very sweet. They have been sold to exclusive restaurants as specialty salads.

225. I must remove many curved fruit from my cucumber plants. Could these be sold?

I am aware of several growers who marketed these curled fruit at a length of four to five inches (10-12 cm). They were packaged in bunches with shrink-wrap. They sold for $1.50 per pound as a specialty product, as they are very tender at that stage of development.

226. I have about half an acre of greenhouses and would like to grow both tomatoes and cucumbers. Is it possible to grow these crops in the same greenhouse?

No. Tomatoes and cucumbers require different temperatures and nutrient formulations. If you have individual greenhouses you can grow tomatoes in one and cucumbers in another. If it is a gutter-connected greenhouse, it is possible to divide the greenhouse with a polyethylene partition. To obtain different temperature regimes it is necessary to have the heating system controlled in two separate zones (hot water heating) or separately operated unit heaters. The nutrient solution must be distributed through separate irrigation systems, including nutrient tanks.

227. What type of equipment is best to shrink wrap cucumbers for an operation one acre in size?

For relatively smaller operations, it is possible to use an L-bar sealer and an oven. Each fruit must be placed in the shrink-wrap of the L-bar sealer, which seals and cuts the wrap around the cucumber. It then passes through an oven, which heats the outside briefly, as it travels through on a belt, causing the wrap to shrink tightly around the fruit.

228. How should cucumbers be packed, and at what temperature should they be stored?

Cucumbers are normally packed 12 or 16 to a box. Grade them as regular, large and jumbo sizes. Do not mix sizes in a box. They should be stored under refrigeration between 50 and 55 F (10-13 C). Stack the boxes on pallets. Before shipping, wrap the outside of the stack with a plastic stretch wrap to stabilize the boxes on the pallet.

Pests, Diseases and Physiological Disorders

229. My neighbor who grows cucumbers and tomatoes says that it is important that everyone, prior to entering the greenhouse, should disinfect their shoes. Is that a good idea?

Yes. A "shoebath" at the entrance to the greenhouses is important in controlling the spread of fungi and bacteria into the houses. Construct a shallow rectangular reservoir the same size as a floor mat, about 2 ft. × 3 ft. (60 × 90 cm), of metal or plastic, to a depth of two inches (5 cm). Keep it filled with a 10 percent bleach solution. You may place an outdoor carpet in it provided that the bleach solution is kept to the top of the mat. Do not forget to add bleach to the footbath every few days. Post a sign calling attention to the "shoebath," with appropriate warning.

It is also a good idea to provide workers with either disposable overcoats or other clothes, which should be washed frequently to prevent the spread of diseases in the greenhouses.

230. I grow cucumbers in Florida where I encounter severe insect and disease problems. They significantly reduce my yields after several months of harvesting. What could be done to overcome these problems?

With the high insect and disease pressures of these regions, it is very difficult to maintain high productivity for many months. Insects often introduce disease, especially viruses that have no cure, so you must depend upon exclusion and control of the insects, as mentioned in *Question No. 201*. Most growers in these areas use short cropping periods, of three months, constantly replacing the plants. It is important in using such a short cycle that you prevent seedlings from becoming infected. Keep the seedlings in an isolated greenhouse, or section well-screened to prevent insects. Partition the greenhouses to keep crops of different ages separated from other older crops. Focus on the winter market window when prices are highest. Do not grow crops from June through September when prices are generally suppressed with high supply. During these months, clean up the greenhouses and prepare for the next crops.

231. Some of my cucumber fruit yellows and have brown tips as they start to develop. Is this a disease, and should they be removed?

This is not a disease. It is abortion of the fruit, as the plant cannot support them all. Remove the aborting fruit very early and reduce the fruit load on the plant by re-moving some of the other fruit. Do not allow any more than two to three fruit to be maturing at the same time. As the fruit load increases, the plant may abort some of the larger fruit, resulting in lost production. This indicates that you must thin the fruit more. High temperatures in excess of 80 F (27 C) also cause fruit abortion.

232. I have found that some of my maturing cucumbers are pointed and have stopped growing. The ends are soft and the fruit will not keep. What is the problem?

If the fruit tip yellows and fails to grow, it is probably aborting due to more fruit on the plant than it can sup-port (see *Question No. 231* above). Other causes could be poor nutrition, light conditions or other unfavorable en-vironmental conditions. Correct the environmental con-ditions and remove some of the fruit. Be sure to remove the malformed fruit early.

233. I find that a lot of the small cucumbers bend or curl. Why is this?

Cucumber fruit curls for a number of reasons. Infesta-tion with thrips in the flowers damages cells in the small, developing fruit. These dead cells cause scars and defor-mation of the fruit. Control the thrips. Changes in envi-ronmental conditions, such as low relative humidity and/or high temperatures, combined with high light will cause curling, often termed "crooking." Any sudden changes in the environment can cause curling. If developing fruit touch leaves or are contacted by tendrils, they will curve. Remove these curved fruit immediately.

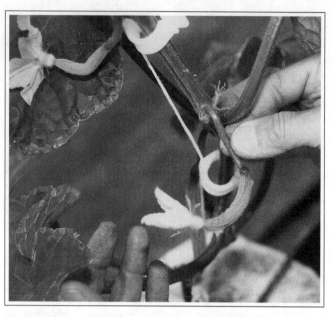

Remove crooked (curved) fruit at an early state, when
they are about an inch long.

234. Sometimes the developing fruit on my cucumbers start to curl when they reach five or six inches (12 to 15 cm) in length. What causes this deformation?

This curving of the fruit, at a later stage, may be a result of any of the above conditions mentioned in *Question No. 233* above. Probably a leaf, tendril or another fruit interfered. Often, as the fruit elongates very rapidly, it may get tangled among other fruit or on leaf petioles. Watch the fruit as they develop and free any that are being interfered with in their growth.

235. I find that some of my mature fruit have scars. What is causing this?

This may be caused by thrips in the flowers, insect larvae chewing the fruit or by movement of the plants. If workers brush by the plants, causing them to move, the fruit may bump into leaf petioles, other fruit or leaves. Warn workers of the delicate fruit and that they must not move the plants a lot when pruning or walking among the plants.

236. My cucumbers suffer from insect and disease problems. Can anything be added to the nutrient solution to help prevent these problems?

European cucumbers are very susceptible to *Pythium* and *Phytophthora* root rots. It has been found that the addition of 100 ppm of potassium silicate to the nutrient solution will strengthen the cuticle covering of plant leaves thus adding resistance to entry of diseases and insects. Silicone, although not an essential element, is accumulated by plants and is needed for cell wall structure. Lettuce also takes up silicone. It assists in prevention of *Pythium* infection.

Other recent studies now support the use of hydrogen peroxide to prevent these root rot diseases in all crops. Between 30 and 50 ppm in the nutrient solution will add oxygen to the roots and reduce algae growth. It is possible that the added oxygen will promote healthy root growth and thus increase resistance against fungal attack.

237. I find small, white-yellow spots on the upper surface of my cucumber leaves and webbing on the undersides. What is causing this damage?

These are typical symptoms of spider mite damage. The mites feed on the tissue and sap. They are mostly located on the undersides of the leaves, piercing plant cells and sucking out the contents. With increasing damage caused by large populations, the leaves turn completely yellow, then brown as they die. The entire plant can die under uncontrolled infestations. As the population increases, the leaves and, eventually, the plant will be covered with webs swarming with mites.

The loss of chlorophyll will reduce plant growth and yields. Once 30 percent of the leaf surface is damaged, a significant reduction in productivity occurs. Mites will fall to the ground and also travel along the overhead support wires to adjacent plants. They can be spread by air movements of their webs, brushing of infected plant material on clothes of workers as they move through the crop. Between crops, when the greenhouse is empty, they will hide in cracks and feed on weeds, etc., or hibernate in these hidden spaces until favorable conditions allow them to become active again and begin laying eggs as the basis for a new population. For this reason, it is important to keep them under control and eliminate them from the crop before removing it. Also, fumigate the house between crops and spray cracks and all sites within and around the greenhouse where the mites may overwinter.

238. Some of the flowers of my cucumbers have streaks on the petals. I cannot see any insects. What is causing this damage, and how may it be controlled?

This is probably damage from thrips. They are very small and difficult to see without the aid of a magnifying glass. They usually are located inside the flowers. They run fairly quickly. One very distinguishing characteristic of thrips is their feathery wings. Attracted by yellow flowers, they feed on leaf undersides, growing tips and flowers, with their rasping mouth parts, causing small dead spots and white, silvery streaks. Feeding between the calyx and forming fruit of cucumbers, they cause curled and distorted fruits. They pierce and suck out the cell contents of surface tissue.

Several predatory mites, including *Amblyseius cucumeris* and *Amblyseius barkeri*, are used to control thrips. Introduce the predators at a rate between 10 and 200 per plant, depending upon the level of infestation, as soon as thrips are seen in the crop. The predatory mites are available in shaker bottles to aid in distributing them evenly throughout the crop, or as paper sachets, which can be hung on the plants. The slow-release packs will last about 6 weeks. Repeat applications until a predator to prey ratio of 1 : 2 is achieved. Monitor the thrips population with yellow or blue sticky cards. Thrips are attracted to blue and they are more easily visible on blue than on yellow.

"BotaniGard," a mycoinsecticide (see *Question No. 121*), is effective on thrips.

239. I find a lot of algae growing between rows of slabs and into the aisles. How can I prevent this?

As mentioned in *Question No. 236,* addition of 30 to 50 ppm of hydrogen peroxide to the nutrient solution will assist in preventing algae growth. However, the main problem with your system is improper construction of aisles and inadequate drainage between rows of slabs. Pack walkways in a convex fashion so water does not run into the aisles. Always cut drainage slits in the slabs on the inside lower edge facing the drainage ditch. Properly form the drainage ditch between the double rows of slabs, using a jig that could be towed by a tractor in larger operations. Of course, this must be done prior to placing the plastic floor barrier.

240. Some of my plants wilt during midday. I found that the roots of these plants have brown tips; others are completely brown. What is happening?

These symptoms suggest *Pythium* infection of the roots. Refer to *Question No. 124* for treatment. It is also important to prevent algae growth around the plants, as indicated above in *Questions No.194* and *239,* as this favors fungus gnats whose larvae eat roots and can transmit *Pythium* to the plants.

241. I have found that some of my cucumber plants have a brown fungus infection on the stems near the base, which, in time, kills the plants. What control can be used for this disease?

This is probably gummy stem blight, often referred to as black stem rot, caused by *Didymella bryoniae.* Be careful not to wound the plants as this parasite enters the plant through stem wounds. It also affects aborted fruit, entering the tips, causing a black jelly-like rot at the tip. It will create brown leaf spots on leaves. It can enter the leaf margins, causing a scorch symptom. Prevent guttation of leaves during the early mornings by ventilation, to lower the relative humidity, as this condition is favorable to fungal infection. Keep the crop clean, as spores spread from plant to plant on debris. The disease can also spread on hands of workers and their tools. Wash and sterilize tools often, as pointed out in *Question No. 201.* Remove infected plants carefully without touching neighboring ones. Place them in a plastic bag immediately for removal from the greenhouse.

Spray or paint fungicides on the base of the plant stem. Rovral 50 WP or Benlate 50 WP and Manzate 200 can be applied at four to seven day intervals, when infection appears, or during high relative humidity with low light conditions. Do not apply within five days of harvesting, *and first check with local agricultural regulations before using any of these on the crop, as some may not be approved in your location.*

242. The leaf margins of some of my cucumber plants are brown. What is the problem?

If it is the margins of only a few plants, you might suspect a disease such as gummy stem blight, mentioned above (*Question No. 241*). If the symptoms are common on most of plants in the crop and generalized over the leaves of the plants, it would suggest a burn by a pesticide or a sunscald. Check your records for recent spray applications. Sunburn may be a result of guttation in the early morning, followed by high sunlight conditions, damaging the leaf margins. Potassium deficiency may also cause marginal necrosis (browning) of lower leaves. Check the location of the symptoms. Are they only on the lower older leaves? If so, it will be necessary to take tissue analyses of some of the leaves to determine the potassium levels.

243. The lower leaves of my cucumbers are all white. The disease is progressing upward. What is the problem, and can it be controlled?

I expect that this is powdery mildew. Small white spots first appear on the upper surface of leaves. They spread in size and to other leaves very quickly. Use resistant varieties such as "Flamingo," "Marillo" and others, as listed in *Question No. 181*. Potassium silicate at 100 ppm should be added to the nutrient solution. However, this is not accepted as a complete control. High humidity favors powdery mildew, so maintain the RH below 80 percent. Burning of sulfur in pots has given some success. *Get instructions for this from your supplier;* it will produce a toxic vapor, so must be handled with care and with proper equipment. Some growers use a spray solution of 1 kg (2.2 lb.) of sulfur plus 1 kg of magnesium sulfate in 1000 liters (265 gal.) of water.

244. The top leaves of my cucumber plants are deformed, as well as some of the fruit. What disease is this and how can I prevent and/or cure it?

This is possibly cucumber mosaic virus. It is the most common virus disease of cucumbers. Symptoms include a pale-green or yellow mosaic on the leaves and fruit. Symptoms first appear on younger leaves, which curl downward and become mottled, distorted, wrinkled, and remain stunted. Fruit are often deformed, mottled and remain small. It is readily spread by aphids from weeds or other crops around the greenhouse. Once infected, plants do not recover. Be careful not to confuse a virus infection with calcium or boron deficiencies, which also occur on the youngest leaves first. A nutritional disorder will generally be visible on most plants, whereas a disease will start in localized areas of the greenhouse and spread from there. The first step is to control sucking insects, such as whiteflies, aphids and thrips, that are vectors (carriers) of numerous viruses. They carry them from plant to plant and from other plants outside of the greenhouse. Use insect screens to prevent them from entering the greenhouse. Eliminate weeds around the greenhouse.

245. I have encountered whiteflies on the top of my cucumber plants, especially on the undersides of the leaves. What control measures can be taken to stop these insects from spreading?

Use the same biological and chemical controls as described in *Questions No.118-121*.

**246. My cucumber crop has many leaves,
making it very difficult to apply pesticides.
I have tried a number of sprayers including
backpack sprayers, but none of them can
penetrate the canopy effectively. What would
you suggest using?**

To penetrate high-density crops such as cucumbers it
is necessary to use a low-volume, high-pressure sprayer
such as a fogger. This machine vaporizes the pesticides
into a fine mist that can penetrate the crop and effectively
contact the entire leaf surfaces. The fogger can be pushed
down every other aisle on a cart to apply the fog. Larger
machines can simply be set into a greenhouse section to
fog the whole area.

*Always be sure to wear approved protective clothing and
an approved respirator, and follow the instructions of the
manufacturer.* If your greenhouse has a fog system to cool
the greenhouses the pesticides may be applied through
the fog cooling system.

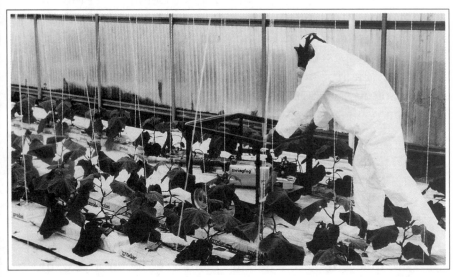

It is important to use protective clothing when applying pesticides, fumigants, etc.,
Here a worker is properly outfitted as he pushes a fogger down the rows on a cart.
Observe the manufacturer's instructions in dispensing these substances. (Courtesy
of Environmental Farms, Dundee, FL.) From the book *Hydroponic Food
Production*, Resh: Woodbridge Press.

Peppers

Cultural Practices

247. I wish to grow a mixture of red, purple, orange and yellow peppers. What are some of the more popular varieties presently in use?

If you wish to grow sweet bell peppers you will want to use the "blocky" types. All the peppers start out as green and change to the final color as they mature. Red varieties include "Cubico," "Mazurka," "Delphin," "Plutona," "Tango," "Delgado" and many more. "Luteus," "Goldstar," "Samantha," "Gold Flame" and "Calvin" are some of the yellow types. Green to orange varieties include "Wonder" and "Eagle." Some of the popular purple varieties are "Violetta," "Mavras," and "Zorro". Consult various seed companies regarding other varieties.

248. When choosing bell pepper varieties, are there special greenhouse types or can I use any of the varieties I have had success with in the field?

You must use the special greenhouse varieties, as they are indeterminate, enabling them to grow for a year, unlike the determinate field varieties that may grow for three to four months. Some of the best greenhouse varieties come from Holland.

249. Should peppers be seeded, similar to tomatoes or to cucumbers in rockwool blocks?

Sow pepper seeds in rockwool cubes, Oasis cubes or round propagation plug trays having a similar 1-inch by 1-inch size. After sowing the seed, cover them with vermiculite to retain the moisture. Soak the rockwool cubes or trays with water of pH 5.2 and an EC of 0.3-0.4 mMho prior to sowing.

250. Are the germination temperatures for peppers the same as those for tomatoes?

Peppers prefer about one degree higher than tomatoes at between 77 and 79 F (25-26 C). To maintain high relative humidity and uniform heat, it is possible to cover the seedling benches with a plastic tent. Do not let the tent rest on the seedling trays, as that will restrict oxygen, which is needed for germination. As soon as the seeds have germinated, remove the tent and lower the air temperature to 72-73 F (22-23 C). Emergence will occur in from seven to ten days.

251. At what age should I transplant my pepper seedlings to the rockwool blocks?

Transplant the seedlings to four-inch (10-cm) rockwool blocks 17 to 18 days after sowing, when the cotyledons are fully expanded. Prior to transplanting, soak the blocks thoroughly with a nutrient solution having pH 5.2 and EC of 2.0-2.2 mMho. Reduce the air temperature slowly to 73 F (23 C), day and night. Space the blocks tightly initially, until the plants grow enough for their leaves to touch. Then you must re-space them, if you are not ready to transplant onto the slabs. In northerly areas, supplementary artificial lighting extending the day length to 18 hours will help produce short, stalky plants. Also, enrich the atmosphere with 800 to 1000 ppm of carbon dioxide.

252. My peppers are six weeks old. Are they ready to transplant to the slabs in the greenhouse?

Peppers are transplanted between seven to ten weeks after sowing, depending upon the available light and plant vigor. The peppers will have to be supported with several stakes while growing in their blocks. Transplanting to the slabs occurs when the plants are about 10 to 12 inches (25-30 cm) tall. At this time the crown bud (flower on node where stem splits into two) should open. This is usually at the fifth to seventh node.

253. I am almost ready to transplant my peppers. What is the recommended spacing of slabs and plant density for peppers?

Plant density in larger operations is about 10,000 plants per acre (25,000 plants per hectare), similar to that of tomatoes. This is equivalent to 4.3-sq. ft./plant (2.5 plants/sq. meter). Grow three plants per slab, spacing slabs apart to obtain within-row spacing of 14 inches (36 cm). Locate double rows of slabs at 16-18 inch (40-46 cm) centers. Slabs for peppers are six inches (15 cm) wide.

254. During transplanting, should the temperatures be changed from that of the seedling area?

The temperatures should be lowered by using a 73-74 F (23-23.5 C) day temperature range, and a night range of 64-65 F (17.5-18 C). Peppers grow slowly, so they require somewhat higher temperatures during early growth.

255. I want to grow a single pepper crop annually. What is the best time to sow seeds?

With a single-cropping system, the most common in northerly areas, sow seed in the propagation house at the beginning of October. By late October, transplant the seedlings to rockwool blocks in the seedling house—still under artificial supplementary lighting. During early December, transplant to slabs or beds in the greenhouse production area. Harvesting will begin in early March and continue until mid-November. From mid-November until the first week of December remove the old plants and clean up the greenhouse.

256. Some growers tell me to train my peppers to two stems; others say three stems are better. What is the most common method of training?

Three stems per plant will reduce the number of plants needed and, therefore, the number of rockwool blocks. The disadvantage is that more labor is needed for training to three stems. The two-stem training system will be described here, as it is the most common method. Training begins as the crown bud forms at the first bifurcation of the plant. Within three to four weeks from transplanting onto the slabs, the plant stems will have to be tied with the support strings. You can use plant clips, combined with wrapping the string around the stems in a clockwise direction, as described for tomatoes. Support the stems in a V-cordon method.

If the overhead wires are high (about ten feet, or three meters) the peppers will not have to be lowered. If a low wire system is used, the plants will have to be lowered as they grow taller, similar to tomatoes; but only three to four times during the year, as they grow much slower than tomatoes. Stems must be trimmed to maintain a balance between generative and vegetative growth. Remove all flowers up to a plant height of 16 inches (40 cm). Once the two stems have formed, prune all sideshoots after the second leaf forms. This suckering will have to be done every two weeks. Allow the first fruit to develop at the third node above the main stem bifurcation. Fruit should ripen within seven to nine weeks after setting. If too many fruit form, remove any small, misshapen fruit. Be careful not to remove too many fruit, or the remaining fruit will size too quickly. This may cause nutrient deficiencies, especially calcium, creating blossom-end-rot.

257. Can peppers be pollinated with bumblebees, as can be done with tomatoes?

Yes. Peppers, like tomatoes, should be pollinated by bumblebees. As discussed in *Questions No. 85* and *86,* be careful that the bees do not overwork the blossoms. An overpopulation of bees in the peppers, overworking the plants, will cause a zipper-pattern scar on the fruit. You require a lower population of bumblebees for peppers than is needed for tomatoes.

258. When my workers harvest the peppers, they break a lot of fruit at the stem. Can they cut the fruit with a knife or will this spread virus diseases?

Harvest the fruit with a sharp knife, making a clean cut. Dip the knife in milk between cuts to prevent the spread of viruses (see *Question No. 201*). Some of the more common viruses of peppers are: Mild Mottle Virus (MMV), Tomato Spotted Wilt Virus (TSWV) and Tobacco Mosaic Virus (TMV).

259. I received about four pounds per square foot of production from my pepper crop. Is this about average?

That yield is slightly below the average of 4.3 to 5 lb./ sq. ft. (20-25 kg/sq. meter). The yield depends somewhat on varieties. Red varieties yield more than yellow ones. High quality fruit should measure between 3 and 3.5 inches (7.5-9.0 cm) at the shoulders. It must be of uniform, blocky shape, with no insect or disease blemishes, skin cracks, blossom-end-rot or other marks.

260. With my pepper crop, I realize that the optimum range for the various environmental conditions is fairly narrow. What are the optimum ranges of temperature, RH, etc. for mature plants?

To maintain a balance between vegetative and generative growth, D. H. Marlow (1993) recommends the 24-hour mean temperature should be close to 68 F (20 C) with day and night temperatures at 72 F (22 C) and 66 F (19 C), respectively. Lower temperatures will favor vegetative growth, slowing fruit maturation. Higher temperatures may cause the plant to become dormant, causing flowers to not set and/or fruit abortion.

Relative humidity should be kept between 75 and 80 percent. Low RH will cause excessive evapotranspiration, causing a water deficit, leading to blossom-end-rot of the fruit. High RH will substantially reduce water uptake and consequently diminish nutrient uptake, leading again to nutritional problems as BER.

Enrich carbon dioxide in the greenhouse atmosphere to a level between 800 and 1000 ppm.

261. The pH and EC of my slab solution are 6.5 and 4.0 mMho respectively. Should this be adjusted, and how?

Both the pH and the EC are too high. Under good light conditions the slab EC should be kept at about 3.0 mMho and the pH at 5.5 to 6.0. The EC of the feed solution would be about 2.0 mMho. Adjust the pH and EC of the slabs, through your formulation and frequency and duration of irrigation cycles, as discussed in *Questions No. 36, 100, 206* and *211*.

262. I realize that under cloudy, low-light conditions, the EC of the slabs should be raised for peppers, but by how much?

In northerly areas that suffer from inadequate light in the late autumn until early spring, it is necessary to raise EC levels. The EC of the slab should be between 2.8 and 3.1 mMho. As light intensity and day length increases, lower the EC to between 2.0 and 2.5 mMho.

263. I am going to install a fog system to cool my plants. Are there any special precautions needed in its use?

Fogging systems are good for increasing humidity and decrease temperatures in the greenhouse. It can also be used to apply pesticides. However, care must be taken not to spread diseases such as mildews, and not to make the plants too soft, leading to susceptibility to some diseases. Sometimes fogging can shock the plants, keeping them vegetative. Fog is good to improve environmental conditions, especially when plants are young (not producing fruit). Once plants grow to a height of four to five feet (1.5 m), they will transpire a lot of water vapor, increasing the relative humidity and decreasing the temperatures in the greenhouse. At that time, less fogging will be required. The fogging system may be controlled, with the assistance of a computer, monitoring the ambient weather conditions.

264. After harvesting my peppers, at what temperatures and relative humidity should they be stored and shipped?

Peppers, as with cucumbers, should be refrigerated at temperatures slightly lower than those for tomatoes—between 45 and 50 F. (7-10 C). They will keep two to three weeks at these temperatures. Maintain relative humidity between 85 percent and 90 percent.

Pests, Diseases
and Physiological Disorders

**265. I have a few whiteflies on my peppers,
controlled by my predators; however, a very
small population still exists. For this reason,
I am concerned about the spread of viruses.
Are there varieties of peppers resistant to
these viruses?**

Most of the greenhouse varieties have resistance to viruses. Most are resistant to TMV and MMV with some having resistance to Potato Y Virus (PVY). Check the specifications of your varieties in the seed catalogs of the suppliers.

**266. After harvesting the fruit of my pepper
plants, I find blossom-end-rot fruit on
plants. How can I avoid this problem?**

Peppers have a delicate balance between fruit and plant growth. If you harvest too much fruit at any given time, it will cause a rapid acceleration of the growth rate of the remaining fruit. This may lead to the plants' inability to supply sufficient nutrients to the rapidly maturing fruit, resulting in blossom-end-rot. Harvest more frequently and less fruit at any one time. Sudden increases in growth rate will lead to BER and skin cracks.

**267. Some of my pepper plants were suffering
from blossom-end-rot. Should I remove the
bad fruit?**

As with tomatoes, it is best to leave the bad fruit on the plant. Removing them could upset the growth rate of the other fruit. As pointed out above in *Question No. 266,* follow cultural practices that will avoid any sudden changes in growth of the remaining fruit.

268 I find some of my peppers get sunscald on the fruit. How can this be prevented?

Peppers are very susceptible to sunscald. Direct sun on fruit will raise the surface temperature, causing rupture of cells, resulting in sunken, watery patches, especially on the shoulders and middle of the fruit. When training the plants, care must be taken not to remove too many leaves, especially those around the fruit. During the summer months it may be necessary to partially shade the greenhouse, using 25-30 percent shading. An automatic shading system, linked to the computer monitoring weather conditions, is ideal to carry out this partial shading during the brightest times of the day (usually noon to 2:00 PM). After several days of cloudy weather, apply the partial shade for longer periods, reducing its use over three to four days as outlined in *Question No. 93*.

269. Blossom-end-rot seems to be a common problem with peppers. What conditions are causing it and how should changes be made to prevent it?

Any conditions that interfere with calcium uptake in the plant will lead to blossom-end-rot. Generally, there are a combination of environmental factors, coupled with water and nutrient uptake, that predispose the plants to calcium deficiency. High or low relative humidity, irregular watering, non-optimum temperatures, excessive solar radiation, insufficient calcium in the nutrient solution or imbalances in the ion ratios of the solution lead to BER. Any cultural or environmental factors that favor sudden flushes in fruit development, as indicated in *Questions No. 260, 266* and *267*, will cause BER. Maintain all of these factors at optimum levels to prevent it.

270. Some of my peppers have large fruit cracks. What is causing this?

Fruit cracks may be caused by sunscald, changes in environmental conditions, irregular watering and other factors related to causing rapid fruit expansion as pointed out in *Question No. 269* above. Varieties differ in their susceptibility to fruit cracking, so choose varieties having resistance to this disorder. Fruit maturing and ripening slowly is more prone to fruit cracking. Avoid sudden changes in and non-optimal environmental conditions that may slow fruit maturation. Do not allow large differences between day and night temperatures, keeping them within the optimal ranges as outlined in *Question No. 260*.

Backyard Greenhouses

271. I am going to construct a backyard greenhouse. Some of my neighbors, who have small greenhouses, tell me to make it larger than 8 ft. × 12 ft. (2.4 × 3.6 m.), as they find in a short time that they run out of space. What size do you think is best?

From my experience in the past as a builder of small hydroponic greenhouses, I found that many customers who purchased small houses of 8 ft. × 12 ft. were short of space within six months. When visiting the company to purchase nutrients, they often remarked, "The only mistake I made was not to buy a larger greenhouse, as I am running out of space." I always recommend that the gardener start with one of at least 10 ft. × 12 ft. (3 × 3.6 m.), and then, if more space is needed, it is relatively easy to extend it without having problems in cooling. The narrower 8-ft. (2.4 m.) width is more difficult to extend beyond 12 feet, as cooling becomes a problem. In addition, the 10-ft. width permits a third bed in the center so the growing area is increased about 30 percent with just the extra two feet in width.

Many people plan on growing only vegetables hydroponically, but before they realize it, they have become so fascinated that they soon wish to experiment with other crops and spend a lot more time growing all sorts of vegetables and ornamentals in the greenhouse.

And, don't forget, whether building or buying a greenhouse, you will probably need a building permit. Check with your local authorities.

272 I am presently constructing my hobby greenhouse and plan to grow tomatoes, cucumber, peppers and lettuce. What varieties would you recommend for hydroponic culture?

Use the same varieties as commercial growers. For tomatoes use "Trust," which is the most popular greenhouse variety in North America. "Blitz" and "Laura" are good for the higher light season of the summer months. Others include "Caruso" and "Match." There are many others to choose from various seed houses. Keep in mind that they must be indeterminate (staking) in nature, so that they will continue growing vertically in your greenhouse. I would suggest that if you have a favorite outdoor variety based upon its flavor, try some in the greenhouse. But, as a general rule, do not use outdoor varieties, as they will probably not yield as well as the specially bred greenhouse varieties. You may wish to grow cluster tomatoes and even cherry varieties such as "Ambiance" (cluster), "Tradiro" (cluster), "Favorita" (cherry) and "Conchita" (cherry).

With cucumbers, grow only the European type, not the normal garden type. These are the seedless, burpless greenhouse varieties, such as "Corona," "Farbio," "Marillo," "Milligon" and "Discover." The latter three are resistant to powdery mildew but require the higher light conditions of the summer months. Some popular varieties of peppers, which are the "bell," or "blocky," type include: "Spartacus" (red), "Cubico" (red), "Plutona" (red), "Goldflame" (yellow), "Kelvin" (yellow), "Samantha" (yellow), "Luteus" (yellow), "Eagle" (orange), "Mavras" (purple), "Purpleflame" (purple), "Zorro" (deep violet), "Choco" (Chocolate brown), "Bianca" (ivory) and "Tequila" (lilac). Obviously, there are many to choose from. Grow what you like in terms of sweetness and color, but you will have better production with the greenhouse indeterminate varieties. There are also many others, such as the longer "lamuyo" types and the hot peppers, which are also available in several colors.

There are many lettuces to consider, such as "Ostinata" (bibb), "Deci-Minor" (bibb), "Cortina" (bibb), "Red Oakleaf," "Cimarron" (red romaine), "Lolla Rossa," "Paris Island Cos" (romaine) and "Tango."

273. I have a small hobby hydroponic greenhouse 10 ft. × 14 ft. (3 × 4.3 m.), growing lettuce, tomatoes and cucumbers. Do I need a different nutrient formulation for each crop?

You would undoubtedly enjoy more optimum yields using separate formulations for each crop. However, for a hobby greenhouse it is not practical to have different tanks, pumps, etc. for different areas growing each crop. Use a general tomato formulation for all of them. I think that tomatoes are likely to be your most important crop, so the best formula for the tomatoes will also serve for cucumbers and lettuce, as it has adequate calcium. The formula will be too high in potassium to permit the lettuce heads to form tightly, but you are using them for yourself so they do not need to meet market standards. The lettuce will be very succulent and tasty, so do not be too concerned. In addition, you will produce more than enough vegetables for yourself and many of your neighbors, so do not be disappointed if your production is somewhat less than is optimally possible.

274. In my backyard greenhouse can I grow lettuce and herbs under my tomato plants?

Yes. The lettuce and herbs will easily grow under the tomatoes once the tomatoes are high enough so that you may remove some of the lower leaves. Seed the lettuce and herbs about three weeks prior to the first fruit trusses on the tomatoes are ready to harvest (about 9-10 weeks after sowing the tomatoes). An earlier crop of lettuce and herbs may be sown at the same time as the tomatoes so that they may all be transplanted together into the beds. The first crop of lettuce will be ready to harvest as the tomatoes are growing (about four weeks after transplanting). The herbs can continue growing, simply cut the tops as you require them.

The lettuce and herbs will be somewhat "soft" and very delicate growing under the tomatoes, as they will become a little "leggy," but this is not a problem since they will still be of excellent quality for your own use. Harvest them just before consuming them, as they will be very delicate and will not keep under refrigeration. Besides, they have much better flavor if not refrigerated. This is also true for tomatoes and cucumbers.

275. How should I pollinate tomato plants in my backyard greenhouse?

While bumblebees would work fine, you cannot purchase a hive small enough for such a greenhouse. A commercial hive has far too many bees for the few plants in your greenhouse. As a result, they would overwork the blossoms and damage the fruit. Pollinating by hand with a vibrator is most efficient and simple. Just be sure to pollinate every day. This should take only about five minutes.

276. I have found whiteflies and other insects in my backyard greenhouse. How should I control them?

While you may use pesticides, it is better to use the biological agents. First, you must identify exactly what the insects are. Purchase a good book having color illustrations of garden insect pests. Once you know what they are, you can buy some predators from various greenhouse supply companies. Be careful that you do not use any chemicals with long persistence before you introduce the predators. See section above under *Tomatoes – Pests, Diseases and Physiological Disorders* for biological agents and compatible pesticides. *Do not use any insecticide, pesticide, fumigant or the like without reading the manufacturer's instructions and checking with your agricultural agent for any local regulations.*

277. In my backyard greenhouse I change the nutrient solution every two to three weeks. Is that okay?

With a backyard greenhouse it is not feasible to have the nutrient solution analyzed, as it costs between $35 and $50 per analysis. You should monitor the pH and EC of the solution with indicator paper and hand-held, relatively inexpensive meters (costing less than $100). Maintaining the pH at levels between 5.5 and 6.3 is important and should be checked daily. The EC also needs to be tested daily and adjustments made for poor light conditions, as pointed out in previous questions. This is only an indication of total dissolved solutes and does not tell you what elements need to be added. The amount of fertilizers used in your nutrient solution is not expensive, so the easiest method of keeping the solution in balance is to change it frequently.

I recommend that you change the solution at least every other week. You may use the spent solution on your lawn, flowers or other vegetables in your backyard. During the winter months in northerly areas, use the spent solution on houseplants.

278 I am building a backyard greenhouse and would like to know what hydroponic system to use?

The simplest systems to use for vine crops, like tomatoes, cucumbers and peppers, are rockwool and perlite. For lettuce and herbs use a NFT gutter system. All systems in a backyard greenhouse should be recirculated. Perlite and rockwool cultures can be recirculated, with the use of plastic or enameled metal trays placed under the bags or slabs. The nutrient tank should be of fiberglass or other rigid durable plastic. Place it in the ground with the ends of the beds located on the top of the tank. In this way you can reduce the amount of plumbing required. You would not need catchment pipes and return pipes to the tank. The beds will have to be raised somewhat to obtain at least a one to two percent slope back to the tank. To protect the beds from the cold ground temperatures place one-inch-thick styrofoam under the return trays.

Be sure to cover the tank with plywood or rigid plastic to prevent exposure of the nutrient solution to light. This will prevent algae growth in the solution.

Hydroponic Home Food Gardens (Resh: Woodbridge) has lots of photographs and information about hydroponic systems and equipment

279. I live in the Pacific Northwest where light during the late fall to early spring is limited due to cloudy conditions. Should I use supplementary artificial lighting during those seasons?

Definitely. Artificial lighting will help your plants during low-light, short-day periods. With these lights, extend the day length to 18 hours. Either eight-foot, cool white fluorescent or high-intensity discharge (HID) lights may be used. These lights may be purchased from hydroponic garden shops, or electrical supply companies. If you prefer to use fluorescent lighting, purchase high output units. HID lamps are mercury halide and sodium vapor units. These are very bright and may upset your neighbors. HID lights cost from $200 and up, depending upon their wattage.

280. I live in Vancouver, B.C., and have a backyard greenhouse. I am growing tomatoes, cucumbers and lettuce. I would like to grow these crops year-round. Is this feasible, and what cropping schedule would you think appropriate for this area?

With the use of artificial lighting as indicated above in *Question No. 279*, it is possible to grow through the cloudy months of the year. However, the yields of tomatoes, cucumbers and peppers will not be as high as during the higher light periods, with only natural sunlight. Normally, you should concentrate on lettuce and herbs during these poor light condition periods. They do not require the high light levels as do fruiting plants such as tomatoes, cucumbers and peppers. Sow seeds of leafy vegetables every week, keeping continuous production.

Sow tomatoes, cucumbers and peppers in late November for transplanting during December. These seedlings could be started in your basement under artificial lights for a period of four to five weeks before moving into the greenhouse. It would be better to start a second crop by early June to get more vigorous plants through the fall months when light starts to decrease. Carry the crop through November.

281. I find that the rockwool slabs are expensive. Is there a simple way to sterilize them so that they could be reused several times?

Yes. They can easily be sterilized, using your stove. After pulling the plants from the slabs remove the plastic wrapper. Set the slabs on edge to drain inside the greenhouse for several days. Once they are dry, place them inside the oven of your stove. Heat them to about 200 F (93 C) for an hour. Test the temperature *inside* one of the slabs to determine that it reaches at least 180 F (80 C), and keep them at this temperature for half an hour. Rewrap the slabs with 6 mil white polyethylene before using them again.

282. I have just removed the plants from my hobby greenhouse. How can I prepare it for the next crop?

You must sterilize all surface areas and all cracks with a 10 percent bleach solution. Use a sprayer to fumigate all of the cracks, floor, walls, etc., as many insect eggs, pupae and fungal spores may be lodged in these areas, overwintering until your next crop is started. They will immediately infect your new crop. *Remember the cautions stated in* Question No. 276 *about using hazardous substances.*

You must also clean all pipes, pumps and tank(s) with a 10 percent bleach solution to kill algae and fungi. Fill the nutrient tank one-third full and make up the bleach solution in it. Pump the solution through the system for half an hour. To unplug drip lines afterwards, make up an acid solution of concentrated battery acid (sulfuric acid), which is available at car supply stores, at a 1:50 dilution. Leave the solution in the lines for 24 hours before flushing with clean water. *Be sure to follow the manufacturer's directions for handling the acid safely. Review again, Question No. 22.*

283. When should I pick my tomatoes from my backyard greenhouse?

Pick them at the red stage, just before you wish to eat them. "Red" indicates that 90 percent of the surface is red. Do not refrigerate tomatoes, as this will reduce their real "backyard" flavor. Snap the fruit off by hand, leaving the calyx intact.

284. I have read that the greenhouse environment should be enriched with carbon dioxide. Is it important to do so with backyard greenhouses?

Carbon dioxide enrichment will increase the productivity of most crops in your greenhouse. However, for a backyard greenhouse, the cost of generating it or buying bottled carbon dioxide is not feasible. Even if yields could be increased by 20 percent, you still obtain more production from your greenhouse than you can consume, even without using enrichment with carbon dioxide.

285. I am constructing my backyard greenhouse. What method of cooling should I install?

The two most common methods are exhaust fans and ridge vents. Forced-air exhaust fans will need several vents on the opposite end of the house. These will open automatically on negative pressure, as the exhaust fan operates from a thermostat. Do not use both ridge vents and exhaust fans as this will short-circuit the air from above rather than forcing it through the crop canopy. Ridge vents are fine to use if they are opened with a thermostat and are sufficiently large to permit the formation of convection currents in the greenhouse, bringing in outside fresh air as the hot air escapes. A fogging system also works well, but is more expensive than the other systems.

286. I wish to grow tomatoes and cucumbers in my hobby greenhouse. Will I need to heat it?

Yes. All the greenhouse varieties of plants are bred to yield highly under high night temperatures. Even during the summer months it may be necessary to heat if the ambient temperature falls below 60 F (16 C). The easiest system of heating is to use an electric space heater or baseboard heater operated by a thermostat. Install a 220-volt electrical service if you can, as this power will be cheaper in the long run than 110 volts. If you have a 220-volt, 200-ampere service in your house you may have sufficient power for your greenhouse. Check with your local building authorities.

287. I suffer from a lot of stress in my profession. An associate told me that he recently bought a backyard greenhouse and finds that it offers an escape for him after work. Have you known other people to experience this?

Yes. This is a common feeling of many people who have taken up the hobby of backyard greenhouse gardening. It is an escape for them, a release of tensions of the day. Many customers have told us that they can completely forget all of their employment problems when they enter their greenhouses. Another feeling people have, especially in the cloudy, dark days of winter in the northerly areas, is that it lifts their spirits.

If they feel depressed, they can get a positive feeling in the warm, humid climate of the greenhouse. If they have artificial lights, this also helps to counter the dark conditions outside.

Closing Remarks

I hope that I have helped you in answering some of the questions you may have regarding hydroponics and the growing of plants, using various cultural techniques. As mentioned at the outset, all biological sciences encounter problems due to the many variables in dealing with living organisms, which respond to their physical and biological environment (nutrition, climate, pests and diseases). I am sure that you have other questions that I have overlooked or have not experienced, as new problems arise continually. Hydroponics, like other sciences, is one which is constantly developing and, in doing so, more problems arise. The science progresses with these problems and solutions to them. So, do not despair when you have a problem. Think that, in studying it and arriving at creative solutions, you are really contributing to the advancement of hydroponics.

References

Bakker, J. C. 1988. Russetting (cuticle cracking) in glasshouse tomatoes in relation to fruit growth. Journal of Horticultural Science, 63: 459-463.

Blancard, D. 1997. A color atlas of tomato diseases, observation, identification and control. Manson Publishing, John Wiley & Sons, New York.

California Tomato Board. Buyer's Guide—Ripening Stages. California Tomato Board, Fresno, CA 93727.

Koppert, B. V., Koppert Side Effect List. Koppert Biological Systems, The Netherlands.

Malais, M. and W. J. Ravensberg. 1992. Knowing and recognizing. Koppert Biological Systems, The Netherlands.

Marlow, D. H. 1993. Greenhouse crops in North America: A practical guide to stonewool culture. Grodania A/S, Milton, Ontario, Canada.

Province of British Colombia, 1993. Greenhouse Vegetable Production Guide. B.C. Ministry of Agriculture, Fisheries and Food, Victoria, B.C., Canada.

Resh, Howard M. 1995. Hydroponic Food Production. 5th ed. Woodbridge Press, Santa Barbara, CA.

Glossary

A

Abscission zone/layer: a natural layer between a leaf and stem where the leaf will separate from the stem, forming a zone of rapid healing with a layer of tissue resistant to infection

Active ingredient: that chemical part of a pesticide (usually a small percentage) which acts in controlling the pest

Aeroponics: a form of hydroponics that applies nutrients to plant roots directly by mist in a closed system

Atomic weight: the relative weight of an atom.

B

Beneficials: insects, fungi, bacteria or nematodes that feed on other pest organisms

Bibb lettuce: a European type of lettuce varieties which form soft, semi heads that are the most popular lettuces grown hydroponically.

Biological agents: biological organisms that control pests (see beneficials).

Biological contaminants: biological organisms present on produce causing diseases to humans consuming the product—e.g. *E. coli* bacterium.

Blossom-end-rot (BER): a physiological and nutritional disorder on fruit creating a black leathery sunken appearance on the blossom end of the fruit—often associated with poor watering, root death, and calcium deficiency

Buffering action: the ability of a nutrient solution or raw water to resist changes in pH, that is, the solution has a stable pH.

C

Calyx: that part of a fruit having small leaf-like form at the stem end opposite to the blossom end of the fruit—especially important in harvesting tomatoes.

Capillary mat: a polyester thin matting, about 1/8-inch thick, used to move a solution laterally along a surface through capillary action similar to a blotter.

Chlorosis: a yellowing of tissue due to a physiological disorder such as a nutrient deficiency.

Cistern tank: a nutrient tank located below ground level so that the solution can return by gravity.

Closed (recirculating) system: a hydroponic system in which the nutrient solution is collected, usually in a solution tank, and then circulated through the system many times.

Controlled ecological life support systems (CELSS): a closed system in the space program to allow astronauts to support their lives through production of food hydroponically and the reuse of waste materials in providing the basic needs to support their lives as part of a small ecological self-sufficient system.

Controlled environment agriculture (CEA): the growing of agricultural crops in structures as greenhouses that permit the regulation of optimum environmental conditions for the crop year 'round regardless of ambient weather conditions.

Cotyledons: these are the seed leaves of a plant, which are the first leaf-like structures that appear during germination, but are not true leaves.

Cropping cycle: the time period during which the plant grows from seeding until final harvest and its subsequent removal.

D

Deep flow/raft culture: a hydroponic system commonly used for lettuce production in hot climates where the plants are supported on top of a bed of nutrient solution by styrofoam boards floating on the solution.

Determinate (bush) varieties: plants that do not continue growing upward but naturally terminate their growth in a bush form having a short cropping period.

Disease organism: a biological organism capable of upsetting the physiology of a plant, causing a reduction in productivity or eventual death.

E

Ebb-and-flow: a hydroponic system in which the plants are sub-irrigated periodically and the nutrient solution drains back to a central cistern for subsequent cycles, a recirculating system.

Electrical conductivity (EC): a measure of the ability of a nutrient solution to conduct electricity, which is dependent upon the ion concentration and nature of the elements present.

Emitter: a device that allows water to drip slowly at a specific location during an irrigation cycle.

Essential elements: mineral elements that are essential for plant growth; the plant cannot complete its normal life cycle without any one of these elements.

Evapotranspiration: the loss of water from a plant through evaporation and transpiration; critical in the uptake of minerals and cooling of the plant through movement of water within the entire plant.

F

Fan-jet: a fan connected to a polyethylene duct mounted in the upper space of a greenhouse which circulates the air within the greenhouse; also introduces fresh air into the greenhouse through motorized louvers to assist in cooling and distributes hot air from unit heaters down the length of the house during heating.

Flower cluster/truss: a group of flowers that form from the stem of tomato plants which when pollinated produce the fruit.

Fruit russetting: tomato fruit may have fine cracks when environmental conditions and fruit development are not optimal.

G

Generative growth: reproductive phase of a plant in which it produces flowers and fruit.

Green shoulder: description given to tomato fruit when the top surface near the calyx remains green while the rest of the fruit turns red.

Growing point: the apex of the plant containing cells multiplying and dividing to result in the growth of the plant.

Guttation: plants having high root pressure under high relative humidity conditions will exude water at their leaf margins through specialized cells.

Gutter NFT: a nutrient film technique water culture system in which plants are grown in small gutters.

H

Harden: by exposing a plant to lower temperatures its growth rate is slowed resulting in thicker leaves and stems that tolerate stress better during transplanting.

Honeydew: secretion of sweet liquid from body of some insects such as aphids.

I

Indeterminate (staking) varieties: plants that are normally trained to continue growing upward and capable of continuous production until they die or are terminated.

Indicator paper: a litmus type paper that changes color with specific levels of acid or base used to check pH.

Indicator solution: a solution that changes color with pH changes.

Injector: a piece of equipment which proportions a concentrated nutrient stock solution with a precise amount of water in a ratio to give the resulting solution the exact nutrient formulation calculated by the operator for feeding his crop.

Integrated pest management (IPM): the use of biological agents and natural pesticides for the control of pests on crops.

Ionic exchange: the exchange of essential elements between plant roots and the surrounding soil or nutrient solution in the case of hydroponics.

Ionic form: an element in its free radical state when dissolved in water; available to plants through ionic exchange by the roots.

L

Leachate: the drainage from a substrate such as perlite, foam, rockwool, peatlite, rice hulls, etc. contained in slabs (sausage-form bags), bags or pots; the spent part of a nutrient solution after passing through the plant roots.

Life cycle: the sequence of events from germination or birth of a living organism to its death.

Low-profile crop: a crop such as lettuce, herbs, etc. which are very short in form.

M

Macronutrient: an essential element required by plants in relatively large amounts.

Micronutrient: an essential element required by plants in relatively small amounts

Mineral deficiency: a disorder produced in a plant when an element is not available in sufficient quantity to meet the plant's needs.

Mineral disorder: a physiological upset in a plant produced by an excess or deficiency of an essential element; initially causes specific symptoms in the plant.

Mineral excess (toxicity): a disorder produced in a plant by an element present in quantities higher than is tolerable by the plant.

Mineral (nutrient) uptake: a mineral (essential element) being taken up (absorbed) by the plant roots; the mineral is in its ionic state in the nutrient solution.

Molecular weight: the relative weight of a molecule.

Movable benches: benches in a greenhouse which can roll sidewise on pipe rollers, usually on a pipe frame support; this allows more efficient use of space.

N

Necrosis: browning of leaf tissue due to a nutritional disorder.

Node: area of plant stem where branches or leaves form.

Nutrient film technique (NFT): a water culture system based upon constant flow of the nutrient solution past the plant roots; must be a thin film of water flowing through the roots to provide adequate oxygenation.

Nutrient formulation: the specific makeup of the nutrient solution with each essential element generally expressed as parts per million (ppm).

Nutrient imbalance: when a nutrient solution does not have the correct ratios of elements and one or more elements may be in excess or deficiency that could lead to a nutritional disorder in the plant.

Nutrient solution: the water solution containing all of the essential plant elements in their correct ratios; the basic nutrient supply to plant roots.

O

Open (non-recirculating) system: a hydroponic system in which the nutrient solution passes only one time past the plant roots; the leachate is not collected and returned to a cistern for repeated irrigations.

Organic molecule: a molecule containing carbon (C), hydrogen (H) and oxygen (O).

Overwintering phase: a phase or part of an organism's life cycle in which it can survive unfavorable environmental conditions or in the case of a disease organism it may be a very resistant structure that can survive without the presence of its host (the plant it lives on).

Oxygenation: the supplying of oxygen; usually refers to the needs of plants' roots.

Oxygen deficit: when oxygen is not supplied in adequate concentration to support normal plant physiological processes.

Ozonation: a method of sterilization of the nutrient solution in closed systems, using ozone as a sterilant.

P

Parts per million (ppm): a dilution factor of one part of one substance in a million parts of another; used to express nutrient formulations and calculations of amounts of various fertilizers to use in a given volume of water; also equivalent to 1 milligram (element) per liter (water).

Peatlite mix: a soilless medium consisting of a mixture of peat, sand, vermiculite and/or perlite

Pesticide free: indicates a product was grown without the use of pesticides during the cropping period of the plant.

Percentage leachate: the amount of runoff from a substrate in comparison to the total amount of nutrient solution applied during an irrigation cycle; expressed as a percentage.

pH: a measure of the acid or base of a solution on a logarithmic scale where 7 is neutral; lower is acid and higher is base.

Photoperiod: the length of dark period during the day which is critical to causing plants to remain vegetative or enter a reproductive state of growth; plants may be short-day, long-day or day neutral.

Photosynthates: the products of photosynthesis in plants; including all metabolites manufactured by the plant through the process of photosynthesis.

Plant uptake: the uptake of water and mineral elements by plant roots.

Pollination: the movement of pollen from the male part of a flower (stamens) to the female part (style and stigma); usually accomplished by wind or insects.

Precipitation: when several chemical compounds react to form a new compound which is not soluble in water and settles to the bottom of a nutrient tank in the form of a white powder.

Predatory-prey balance: a balance between populations of the predators and prey; this is the objective of integrated pest management (IPM).

R

Receptive flower: when a flower of a plant is ready to be pollinated.

Retranslocate: the ability of an element to move from one location in a plant, usually the older part, to another site (often the growing point); translocated via the vascular system of the plant.

Reverse osmosis (RO): equipment used to remove minerals from water; water is forced through a differentially permeable membrane by pressure; the mineral elements cannot pass through the membrane.

Rockwool: a substrate used to grow plants hydroponically; an extruded wool-like product formed through a process of melting rock and extruding it in threads and pressing it into loosely woven sheets at high temperatures.

Root absorption: the absorption of essential elements by the roots of plants from the nutrient solution.

Rooting hormone: a powder containing talc and a plant hormone such as indolebutyric acid (IBA) or indoleacetic acid (IAA) is applied to the base of shoot cuttings to assist in their forming roots under a misting system.

S

Sepals: the green outer petals of a flower protecting the inner petals.

Shoot cuttings: the upper 2 to 3 inches of the growing tip of a plant is cut close to a node and dipped in a rooting hormone before placing in a peatlite medium under mist to form roots.

Slab: a plastic bag (about 6-8" wide by 3-4" deep by 40" long) containing rockwool, foam, perlite or sawdust medium for the growing of vine crops.

Solubility: the ability of a fertilizer to dissolve in water to form a solution.

Solution analysis: laboratory analysis of a nutrient solution or water to determine all elements present and their concentrations; results indicate adjustments needed to make in the solution to keep it in balance.

Start tray: a tray used in a rockwool culture system which indicates the level of moisture in the slab and automatically starts an irrigation cycle when the moisture level reaches a preset value.

Sticky cards: cards having a sticky compound on them to attract insects; a method of monitoring the insect populations in a greenhouse; usually yellow in color, but some are blue for thrips.

T

T-tape: a specific type of drip irrigation tubing used with row crops.

Tissue analysis: a laboratory analysis of plant tissue to determine the levels of essential elements present in the plant

Total dissolved solutes (TDS): the concentration of all the elemental ions present in a nutrient solution; electrical conductivity (EC) is a measure of total dissolved solutes. Expressed generally as mMho (millimhos)

Transplants: these are seedling plants at an age when they are ready to transplant from the seedling to the growing/production area.

Transplant shock: during transplanting, plants undergo stress or shock which sets their growth back for days or possibly a week or more until new roots form and the plant can begin to accumulate photosynthates for growth and development.

U

Unit heater: a heater generally mounted in the upper space of a greenhouse on an end wall coupled with a fan-jet system to blow the heated air down the length of the greenhouse; usually gas fired, but also can act as a heat exchanger for a hot water system.

V

Vapor pressure deficit (VPD): is the difference between the actual concentration of water vapor in the air and the maximum possible concentration at a given temperature; it is high under low relative humidity (RH).

Vegetative growth: plant growth that is usually very succulent without producing much fruit as the plant is not in a reproductive state.

Viability of seed: the ability of seed to germinate generally expressed as percent germination.

Vine clip: a plastic hook with a hinge on the back which attaches to the support string allowing it to secure the plant from falling; used on plants that are trained vertically such as tomatoes, cucumbers and peppers.

Vine crops: crops that are trained vertically in the greenhouse requiring vertical support with strings and vine clips.

W

Water deficit: when available water to the plant is insufficient to provide the plant with at least the same amount as is lost by the plant during evapotranspiration; as this deficit of water continues it will cause the plant to wilt.

Weed mat: a woven plastic matting which will prevent weeds from growing when placed on a soil or other medium having viable weed seeds present.

Topical Index

Other books by the author:

Hydroponic Food Production, Fifth Edition. A comprehensive guidebook for professional growers and advanced home gardeners. Large format, hard cover, 527 pages, more than 400 photographs, drawings and tables—plus directories, addresses, references, bibliography, index. $49.50.

Hydroponic Home Food Gardens. Scores of photographs, drawings and diagrams make it easy to have a variety of gardens—a simple home hydroponic window, a deck tray, containers, full-scale hydroponic gardens, or small, home greenhouse projects. 208 pages. $12.95.

Hydroponic Tomatoes for the Home Gardener. Step-by-step directions for producing superior, home-grown tomatoes. Profusely illustrated. 144 pages. $9.95.

Woodbridge Press, P.O. Box 209, Santa Barbara, California 93102.